T0341516

ESSENTIALS OF

Qualitative
Meta-Analysis

Essentials of Qualitative Methods Series

ESSENTIALS OF

Qualitative
Meta-Analysis

Ladislav Timulak
Mary Creaner

 AMERICAN PSYCHOLOGICAL ASSOCIATION

Published by
American Psychological Association
750 First Street, NE
Washington, DC 20002
https://www.apa.org

Order Department
https://www.apa.org/pubs/books
order@apa.org

In the U.K., Europe, Africa, and the Middle East, copies may be ordered from Eurospan
https://www.eurospanbookstore.com/apa
info@eurospangroup.com

Typeset in Charter and Interstate by Circle Graphics, Inc., Reisterstown, MD

Printer: Sheridan Books, Chelsea, MI
Cover Designer: Anne C. Kerns, Anne Likes Red, Inc., Silver Spring, MD

Library of Congress Cataloging-in-Publication Data

Names: Timulak, Ladislav, author. | Creaner, Mary, author.
Title: Essentials of qualitative meta-analysis / Ladislav Timulak and Mary Creaner.
Description: Washington, DC : American Psychological Association, [2023] |
   Series: Essentials of qualitative methods | Includes bibliographical references. |
Identifiers: LCCN 2022016737 (print) | LCCN 2022016738 (ebook) |
   ISBN 9781433838484 (paperback) | ISBN 9781433838491 (ebook)
Subjects: LCSH: Meta-analysis. | Psychology--Qualitative research.
Classification: LCC R853.M48 T56 2023 (print) | LCC R853.M48 (ebook) |
   DDC 610.72/1--dc23/eng/20220602
LC record available at https://lccn.loc.gov/2022016737
LC ebook record available at https://lccn.loc.gov/2022016738

https://doi.org/10.1037/0000313-000

Printed in the United States of America

10 9 8 7 6 5 4 3 2 1

Contents

Series Foreword

Qualitative approaches have become accepted and indeed embraced as empirical methods within the social sciences, as scholars have realized that many of the phenomena in which we are interested are complex and require deep inner reflection and equally penetrating examination. Quantitative approaches often cannot capture such phenomena well through their standard methods (e.g., self-report measures), so qualitative designs using interviews and other in-depth data-gathering procedures offer exciting, nimble, and useful research approaches.

Indeed, the number and variety of qualitative approaches that have been developed are remarkable. The question for many of us, though, has been how to decide among approaches and how to learn the different methods.

Many prior descriptions of the various qualitative methods have not provided clear enough descriptions of the methods, making it difficult for novice researchers to learn how to use them. Thus, those interested in learning about and pursuing qualitative research need crisp and thorough descriptions of these approaches, with lots of examples to illustrate the method, so that readers can grasp how to use the methods.

The purpose of this series of books, then, was to present a range of qualitative approaches that seemed most exciting and illustrative of the range of methods appropriate for social science research. We asked the leading experts in qualitative methods to contribute to the series, and to our delight, they accepted our invitations. Through this series, readers have the opportunity to learn qualitative research methods from those who developed the methods and/or who have been using them successfully for years.

We asked the authors of each book to provide context for the method, including a rationale, situating the method within the qualitative tradition, describing the philosophical and epistemological background, and noting the key features of the method. We then asked them to describe in detail the steps of the method, including the research team, sampling, biases and expectations, data collection, data analysis, and variations on the method. We also asked authors to provide tips for the research process and for writing a manuscript emerging from a study that used the method. Finally, we asked authors to reflect on the methodological integrity of the approach, along with the benefits and limitations of the particular method.

This series of books can be used in several different ways. Instructors teaching courses in qualitative research could use the whole series, presenting one method at a time to expose students to a range of qualitative methods. Alternatively, instructors could choose to focus on just a few approaches, as depicted in specific books, supplementing the books with examples from studies that have been published using the approaches and providing experiential exercises to help students get started using the approaches. Other researchers will just use one book as they strive to master one qualitative method.

In this book, Ladislav Timulak and Mary Creaner explain qualitative meta-analyses. For years, a critique of qualitative research was the absence of a way to aggregate findings across studies. Now that the field has matured and many studies have been conducted, researchers have begun to develop methods for aggregating the findings from these studies. Given their considerable experience conducting qualitative research, as well as qualitative meta-analyses, Timulak and Creaner are well positioned to help us understand how to conduct a qualitative meta-analysis. Their many examples will help prepare readers to conduct meta-analyses and thus advance the field even further.

—*Clara E. Hill and Sarah Knox*

ESSENTIALS OF

Qualitative
Meta-Analysis

1 QUALITATIVE META-ANALYSIS: ITS ORIGINS AND RATIONALE
Situating Our Perspective

Qualitative research has historically been undervalued and marginalized as a research paradigm in psychology. This started to change in the 1980s, and, since then, the number of qualitative studies has grown exponentially, and qualitative research has become a firm part of the scientific discipline. The American Psychological Association (APA) series Essentials of Qualitative Methods and the recent APA guidelines on reporting qualitative research in psychology (Levitt, 2019; Levitt et al., 2018) attest to this development. The growth of qualitative studies in psychology (and other fields) also has brought with it a need to synthesize this expanding number of studies.

This backdrop brings us to the rationale for this book, which comprises an examination of the methods for accumulating findings from qualitative studies. With a growing number of investigations of the same or similar phenomena, scholars and researchers need to find a way to make sense of the body of studies and the accumulated findings. *Qualitative meta-analysis* (QMA), a method of synthesizing the findings of studies that have examined a particular domain of investigation, offers such an opportunity. QMA uses a rigorous, systematic approach to synthesizing and interpreting findings accumulated across individual primary (original) qualitative studies that

https://doi.org/10.1037/0000313-001
Essentials of Qualitative Meta-Analysis, by L. Timulak and M. Creaner

have investigated the same (or similar) phenomena (Timulak, 2009, 2014). In essence, a QMA is a secondary analysis of the primary qualitative studies' findings that are relevant to the specific QMA's designated domain of investigations (Schreiber et al., 1997; Timulak, 2009). QMA also involves assessment of the qualitative methods used in the original primary studies and their impact on the findings of those primary studies. This, in turn, will influence the findings of the specific QMA that analyzed those primary studies (Paterson et al., 2001; Timulak, 2009, 2014).

QMA allows for a summative picture of a field of inquiry that can be a stimulus for the further advancement of knowledge, research, and teaching. A QMA can also have a practical applicability in serving as a basis for guidelines for practice. In applied fields, such as psychotherapy, cumulative knowledge can inform the guidelines for service provision and training. The utility of and rationale for a QMA is therefore twofold—first, in providing a summative and comprehensive picture of a field of inquiry that goes beyond an individual study and, second, in providing a clear, rigorous, and replicable method for producing such a comprehensive picture.

The QMA method we present in this book draws on our experiences of conducting QMAs and, more broadly, on our experiences of conducting qualitative research. It also draws on our knowledge of the methodological writing of other researchers on qualitative research methods in general and QMAs in particular. It is important to note that our use of QMA is influenced by the areas of research in which we are active, in particular psychotherapy. Psychotherapy research has a unique tradition in terms of what is considered good qualitative research and what are acceptable research practices, and this has definitely shaped our account of qualitative research and our approach to QMA.

Specifically in the context of this book and QMA, psychotherapy has a long tradition of quantitative meta-analyses (indeed, the very first ones were conducted on psychotherapy outcomes; M. L. Smith & Glass, 1977) as well as a long tradition of systematic reviews. QMA and quantitative meta-analysis are similar in that both seek to provide a synthesis that extends beyond the findings of individual primary studies and in that both endeavor to assess the impact on those findings of various aspects of the primary studies. Psychotherapy is also a discipline embedded in practical application that is central to mental health provision and involves important stakeholders (e.g., funders, clients, other nonpsychotherapy mental health providers, broader society). This context shapes which research designs (e.g., randomized controlled trials) and methods are considered relevant and likewise shapes our thinking and how we communicate about research.

Finally, before we discuss the specifics of QMA, we note that a meta-analytic approach to the findings and methods of the primary (original) qualitative studies may be referred to in the literature by terms other than QMA. These terms, such as *qualitative metasynthesis* (the most dominant term in the literature, in particular in the discipline of nursing), *meta-ethnography, meta-study*, and others (see the Origins and Overview of Qualitative Meta-Analysis section), either denote procedures shared by various approaches to QMA or denote a specific method of QMA. However, we use the term *meta-analysis* (see Timulak, 2009, 2014) because it comes to us naturally as a continuation of the original term *meta-analysis* that refers to QMA.

OUR JOURNEY TO QMA

Before we outline the history and current status of QMA and our approach to the QMA method, we each share our personal journey of how we came across the use of this method. We are colleagues in one department, and so we have shared a good portion of this journey together.

Laco's Journey

I (Laco—which is short for *Ladislav* and is pronounced "Latso") distinctly remember when the idea of QMA first crossed my mind: It was during the annual conference of the Society for Psychotherapy Research in 2003 in Weimar, Germany. In Weimar, I attended a session in which distinguished qualitative psychotherapy researchers whose work I deeply admired, John McLeod and Clara Hill (Clara is one of the editors of this APA series), commented that as the number of qualitative research studies on psychotherapy is growing, it starts to become a challenge to accumulate and review them. I was sitting in the audience and thought that it should not be so challenging because, as in the case of quantitative meta-analysis, we could treat the results of individual studies as data and analyze them together in a sort of "meta" study. I then tried to apply this idea to the significant-events studies and their helpful impacts because this was the area of research in which I was heavily involved at that time. I presented this early meta-analysis the following year, at the next annual meeting of the Society for Psychotherapy Research, in Rome. This time, John McLeod was in the audience, and he encouraged me to pursue this line of work, although he was cautious about the potential limitations of the method. If I remember correctly, he wondered whether the nuanced approach of qualitative research might become obscured or get lost in this more comprehensive and generalizing approach to qualitative data.

I then submitted this early meta-analysis to *Psychotherapy Research*, and it was eventually published (Timulak, 2007). However, during the review process one of the reviewers noted that I had written up the method in an ahistorical manner, as though I had invented it. This led me to search the literature, and I discovered that QMA as a method had been used in the literature for more than 20 years (since the late 1980s); in fields like nursing, it was a very well-established method, with special issues of journals often devoted to it (most often under the name *qualitative metasynthesis*; Thorne et al., 2004). I then spent an exciting few weeks acquainting myself with all of that literature. Since then, I have conducted several QMAs and written a few methodological papers and chapters about QMA, mainly for psychotherapy and psychology researchers. My involvement in various QMAs taught me about the power of this method as I observed that at the end of each QMA I felt confident that my understanding of the field that QMA was trying to cover (e.g., the clients' experience of therapy) deepened and became conceptually clear and coherent. What I learned from these QMAs inform the current book, and many of the examples we present herein come from those studies. Mary and I conducted several of these QMAs together, and hence we teamed up for this book, which aims to provide a how-to guide for QMA.

Mary's Journey

Given my academic and professional background (i.e., initially education, English literature, philosophy, and subsequently psychological therapy and clinical supervision), it is perhaps unsurprising that I am drawn to knowledge building and meaning seeking from individual stories, experiences, words, texts, and metaphors. My interest and curiosity in this context brought me quite naturally to qualitative research as a personally and professionally congruent approach.

My first introduction to QMA was as an early-career researcher via an invitation from Laco to contribute to a QMA of the outcomes of person-centered/experiential therapies (Timulak & Creaner, 2010). In essence, the undertaking was an apprenticeship training opportunity with Laco in QMA and very much a learning-by-doing endeavor. I subsequently was invited to join his research team for a British Association for Counselling and Psychotherapy–commissioned QMA on eating disorder treatment (Timulak et al., 2013), and since then we have coauthored an article on the experiences of using QMA and, more recently, a chapter on QMA research design. Since then, I have conducted research supervision for several QMA projects with the Counselling Psychology doctoral program and the Master's in Clinical Supervision program at Trinity College, Dublin. I recall being drawn to the pragmatic and systematic nature of the QMA approach and continue to value optimizing the findings from existing research for knowledge building and doing so in a manner that capitalizes on research resources (Malterud, 2019). Using the QMA method has heightened my appreciation of qualitative research in general and the rich cumulative metaperspective that a QMA can provide for researchers and clinicians.

ORIGINS AND OVERVIEW OF QUALITATIVE META-ANALYSIS

QMA (specifically using the name *qualitative meta-analysis*) appears to have been used for the first time by Stern and Harris (1985), who analyzed seven qualitative studies on self-care paradigms among nurses. Schreiber et al. (1997) offered an early definition of QMA as being *"the aggregating of a group of studies for the purposes of discovering the essential elements and translating the results into an end product that transforms the original results into a new conceptualization"* (p. 314; italics in original).

The work of Noblit and Hare (1988) in the field of education also was highly influential in the development of QMA. They outlined their approach to a comparison and synthesis of studies that had investigated similar events, situations, and cases and named their method *meta-ethnography*. They described several applications of their method (e.g., translating one study into another, examining studies that yield contradictory interpretations), which they referred to as a *lines-of-argument synthesis*, and this use of their approach is the closest to the approach to QMA we present in this book. Lines-of-argument synthesis was intended to be used for synthesizing qualitative studies with a similar focus that could potentially contribute to a more comprehensive picture (a discovery of the whole among a set of parts; Noblit & Hare, 1988, p. 63). Noblit and Hare saw inspiration in Glaser and Strauss's (1967) grounded theory approach to systematically comparing similarities and dissimilarities in primary studies and providing a new synthesis and interpretation. Noblit and Hare's method not only was used by other authors (e.g., Atkins et al., 2008), but it also served as an inspiration to other methodologists who developed their own variants of QMA (e.g., Jensen & Allen, 1996).

The field of nursing, which has a prolific qualitative research focus, has brought much innovation and experience in terms of QMA development. There are several types of overlapping methods, some of which use their own terminology and have a "brand name" that captures their unique approach to QMA. Among them, Kearney (1998), a grounded theory researcher in the field of nursing, built on the work of Glaser and Strauss (1967) and presented an approach to QMA called *grounded formal theory*. In her approach, Kearney

calls for meta-analyzing studies that have examined the same or similar phenomena (e.g., experiences of a physical disability) to determine what can be
abstracted as being relevant to several contexts (e.g., what common features
are reported in studies that have examined various physical disabilities?).
Kearney highlights the fact that her approach to QMA parallels the work of
Glaser and Strauss. In their approach, Glaser and Strauss first established a
substantive theory (e.g., dying in hospital), that is, the theory that unfolded
from their data. They then wanted to see whether this theory would be appli-
cable to other contexts and similar phenomena and referred to this as *formal
theory* (e.g., dying in different contexts). An example of Kearney's approach
can be found in her meta-analytic study of women's experiences of domestic
violence across varied ethnic and geographic contexts (Kearney, 2001).

Also working within the nursing context, Paterson et al. (2001) found their
inspiration for naming their approach in sociology, in particular in the work
of the sociologist Zhao (1991). They refer to their approach as *meta-study*,
a method that describes how to analyze and synthesize data from various
studies, including the methods and theories used in those studies. Thus, their
meta-study method has three main features: (a) analysis of the findings from
the primary studies (they refer to this part of their meta-study approach as
meta-data-analysis), (b) analysis of the methodological characteristics of the
primary studies and their influence on the results of the meta-analysis (they
refer to this part of their meta-study as *meta-method*), and (c) assessment of
the theoretical background and the sociohistorical context of the analyses
present in the primary studies (they call this aspect of their method *metatheory*). Paterson et al.'s approach is popular in the literature, and readers can
find varied examples that use the meta-study method either in full or at least
aspects of it (e.g., Paterson et al., 2003).

Other methodologists from the nursing tradition, Sandelowski and Barroso
(2003), presented their approach to QMA in a method they call *metasummary*.
They argue that the metasummary approach to QMA is more descriptive than
other approaches we have mentioned, and it primarily focuses on extracting
findings from the primary studies and counting the frequency of repeated and
similar findings across the primary studies, as well as assessing the importance of an individual study in shaping the final metasummary. A relatively
recent example of the use of metasummary in the field of nursing is Herber
et al.'s (2017) study of the barriers and facilitators to self-care among heart
failure patients.

In addition, in a health research context, Thomas and Harden (2008) used
a method called *thematic synthesis*. In the first stage of their meta-analysis,
Thomas and Harden develop descriptive themes that summarize the findings
of the original qualitative studies. In a later stage, they develop analytical

themes that they typically use to attempt to answer a research question that a particular thematic synthesis is seeking to answer. In their example, which involved a meta-analysis of qualitative studies on children's healthy eating, Thomas and Harden differentiate between *descriptive themes*, which summarized the findings of the primary studies (e.g., a theme could be a finding that children want to assert their independence and may break rules about healthy eating), and *analytical themes*, which tried to highlight what is most important if one wants to encourage healthy eating in children. On the basis of the number of published studies that took this approach, the thematic synthesis approach appears to be a popular form of QMA (e.g., van Leeuwen et al.'s [2019] study on the meaning of quality of life to older adults).

There are several other approaches to systematic reviews that involve elements of QMA because they may also include primary qualitative studies in their analysis, although they also involve other types of studies. These approaches can be at times grouped with QMA in the literature. These methods include *mixed-method systematic reviews* (Pearson et al., 2015), *critical interpretive synthesis* (Dixon-Woods et al., 2006), and *realist synthesis* (Pawson et al., 2005). We mention these for the reader's interest, but we do not focus on them in this book.

Before we embark on situating the approach to QMA we present in this book, we would like highlight other books in this area that typically are located in the field of nursing (and general health research) that readers can consult (e.g., Finfgeld-Connett, 2018; Malterud, 2019; Paterson et al., 2001; Sandelowski & Barroso, 2006). An important resource for the psychology community is a chapter by Sandelowski (2012) in the *APA Handbook of Research Methods in Psychology* and, more recently, Collins and Levitt's (2021) chapter in *Qualitative Research in Psychology: Expanding Perspectives in Methodology and Design*. The recent APA guidelines for reporting qualitative research in psychology also include a section on QMA (Levitt et al., 2018). Furthermore, there are ever-increasing accounts of QMA in the field of psychotherapy (e.g., Hill et al., 2012; Levitt, 2018; Timulak, 2009).

A GENERIC DESCRIPTIVE-INTERPRETIVE APPROACH TO QUALITATIVE META-ANALYSIS

We refer to the approach to QMA that we present in the remaining chapters of this book as a generic *descriptive-interpretive* approach to QMA. Our conceptualization assumes that the QMA procedures we describe can be used in a way that may oscillate between applying a more *descriptive* approach, wherein the meta-analysts lean on more summarizing findings of the primary studies (see Sandelowski & Barroso, 2003), or applying a more *interpretive* approach, in which the meta-analysts outline their theoretical perspective, examine theoretical perspectives of the original/primary researchers, and try to interpret the findings of the original studies from the meta-analysts' theoretical perspective. We assume that QMA studies may be located anywhere on this continuum from description to interpretation. In any case, we firmly believe that the researchers' (here meta-analysts') personal, professional, and theoretical background is a central part of any qualitative research endeavor (here QMA). We argue that a transparent positioning of the meta-analysts is then crucial for the process of a QMA. Together with Stiles (2007), we recognize the place of theory in any research, including qualitative and QMA research (see also Hissa & Timulak, 2020). We elaborate further on this in Chapter 4 in our description of meta-analytic data analysis.

Readers may note a parallel between our description of QMA and the generic descriptive-interpretive qualitative research outlined by Elliott and Timulak (2021). We follow Elliott and Timulak's (2005, 2021) argument that many brand name qualitative research methods (e.g., grounded theory [Levitt, 2021], the interpretative phenomenological approach [J. A. Smith & Nizza, 2021], consensual qualitative research [Hill & Knox, 2021]) share many of the same or similar procedures that essentially help to describe and interpret the studied phenomenon. Elliott and Timulak (2005, 2021), in their "generic" description of descriptive-interpretive qualitative research, draw on many procedures from varied brand name methods that they found useful in their capacity as researchers and as reviewers and readers of qualitative research. They described a set of procedures that do not have to be necessarily adhered to fully or prescriptively by researchers applying a generic approach; instead, they may be considered as a source of inspiration for a specific study. As they argued, although the researchers' theoretical and methodological background is always present, the research problem at hand will pose challenges that they will need to creatively address. The "generic" qualitative procedures that they outlined then serve as a starting point and provide overall general guidelines that the researchers may need to consider.

In a similar manner, in this book we propose a generic approach to QMA. Although we are aware that there are several brand name QMA approaches (we listed some of them earlier in this chapter), we argue that they overlap significantly (e.g., each of them uses the findings from the primary studies as the data, which are then broken into units that are clustered together into themes or categories on the basis of similarities). In addition, some of the idiosyncratic nuances of these brand name approaches to QMA (e.g., some may analyze the theoretical frameworks that are explicitly or implicitly present in the primary studies) may serve as an inspiration for useful cross-fertilization among the approaches themselves. In the chapters that follow, we present our perspective, which is informed by our research experience and professional background. Nonetheless, we want to encourage meta-analysts who wish to use this book as a guide for conducting QMA to creatively adapt the procedures we present, while striving for a high methodological integrity of their QMA.

Similar to Elliott and Timulak (2021), we embrace a *critical realist* stance in which we attempt to offer a transparent, rigorous, and articulate position for studying what is "out there" while being aware of and open about the many limitations of our endeavor. Together with the arguments outlined by Elliott and Timulak, we also see ourselves as having a *dialectical constructivist* approach that acknowledges that our acts of pursuing knowledge shape what we find, change us, and have an impact on what we study, and therefore the process of research is inherently dialogical. In the case of QMA, this dialogical approach involves two levels: (a) the interaction of the primary researchers with their data and (b) the meta-analysts' interaction with their data, that is, the findings of the primary studies (this includes the interaction of the primary researchers with their data).

SUMMARY

In this chapter, we have provided an overview of the origins of QMA and the variations of QMA that have been developed. We discussed the specifics of those overlapping approaches as well as their distinct features. We also provided an orientation for readers about where we situate ourselves as methodologists and researchers within this tradition and described our descriptive-interpretive approach to QMA in the context of those various approaches.

2 DEFINING THE RESEARCH PROBLEM AND PLANNING THE STUDY

Every research study, and every qualitative meta-analysis (QMA), starts with thinking about a potential research problem. There may be many reasons and motivations involved in this process. The process of formulating a research problem or question optimally is led by the meta-analyst's curiosity and motivation to gain a more comprehensive picture of a field of study. This motivation assumes that meta-analysts have knowledge of the field and are aware of an accumulating body of qualitative studies in it. It may also be the case that the meta-analyst is aware of a previous QMA that is now outdated, and a new QMA can be considered (France et al., 2016).

In reality, a QMA may be initiated for more pragmatic reasons. It may, for example, be led by a motivation to try out the method. This was the reason why Laco attempted his very first meta-analysis (Timulak, 2007). A QMA may be also commissioned by an important stakeholder who wants to establish what is known in a particular area from a perspective of qualitative studies in that area. For example, we were commissioned, along with some colleagues, by the British Association for Counselling and Psychotherapy as QMA methodologists to help with a QMA on helpful and unhelpful aspects of eating disorder treatment (Timulak et al., 2013).

https://doi.org/10.1037/0000313-002
Essentials of Qualitative Meta-Analysis, by L. Timulak and M. Creaner
Copyright © 2023 by the American Psychological Association. All rights reserved.

A QMA may be also led by the prospective meta-analysts' awareness, because of their knowledge of the field, of a body of studies that have investigated the same phenomenon that would be useful to analyze because they likely constitute a meaningful whole that could contribute to the knowledge base. For instance, the awareness that there are a number of intensive qualitative significant-events studies that have investigated processes leading to client insight led Timulak and McElvaney (2013) to conduct a QMA on clients' and therapists' processes in studies of insight events in psychotherapy.

Other reasons why a QMA is initiated may include the researchers' motivation to contribute to summative accounts relevant to the delivery of psychological interventions. For instance, we, as humanistic–experiential therapists, were asked to contribute to a volume gathering all types of evidence (e.g., randomized controlled trials [RCTs], quantitative process–outcome studies) on humanistic–experiential therapies with a QMA on clients' experiences of outcomes of these types of therapies (e.g., Timulak & Creaner, 2010). A further motivation for a QMA may be to address something that was examined through QMA in one particular context, for instance, clients' experiences of individual therapy (Levitt et al., 2016), in another context (e.g., in the context of couples therapy; Madden & Timulak, 2022).

Another possible reason to pursue a QMA may be to examine a body of qualitative studies in a particular area in order to develop a quantitative measure whose items are based on a comprehensive conceptualization of a specific phenomenon (e.g., metacategories from a QMA). For instance, Laco was involved in a meta-analysis of helpful and unhelpful impacts reported in significant-events studies of psychotherapy (Ladmanová et al., 2021) for which the ultimate motivation was to develop a measure on the client-reported in-session impacts in therapy (a measure is currently in development by a colleague, Tomáš Řiháček).

There also may be other, at times more pragmatic, reasons for conducting a QMA. For instance, during the COVID-19 pandemic we learned that QMAs may represent a viable option for dissertation projects because they do not depend on the collection of fresh data from participants, which was constricted by public health restrictions. Thus, we suggested several dissertation projects that would perhaps otherwise not have been such a priority for us personally.

THE PERSON OF THE META-ANALYST

All of these examples are just some of the possibilities that may inspire meta-analysts' work. In any case, we believe that the meta-analysts (or at least some members of the team conducting a QMA) need to have solid knowledge of the field in which they want to conduct a QMA because they need to have some sense of whether there is a sufficiently large body of studies to be meta-analyzed. They also need to determine whether there is a potential relevant research problem that needs to be resolved. For instance, our knowledge of the psychotherapy research field, and our awareness that a number of studies have examined client-reported significant events that may have a cumulative value, led to a number of QMAs on significant events and their impact in therapy (e.g., Ladmanová et al., 2021; Timulak, 2007; Timulak & McElvaney, 2013).

Similarly, our knowledge of the discipline of psychotherapy makes us aware that there is a clear rationale for the usefulness of finding out about outcomes of therapy. We know a lot from RCTs that have used standardized measures on whether particular therapies work, but these measures are typically based not on client perceptions but on professionals' conceptualizations of mental health distress and its resolution. This professional perspective can be nicely complemented by the perspectives of clients who report in an open-ended manner (e.g., as a response to questions such as "Has anything changed for you since therapy ended that you would attribute to therapy?"). Thus, we as meta-analysts can check to see whether any qualitative studies have attempted to address this type of question and, if there are, note what they cumulatively found, perhaps leading to a robust reason for conducting a QMA on client-reported outcomes of psychotherapy (Timulak & Creaner, 2010).

We also believe it is important that the prospective meta-analyst has knowledge of qualitative methods so they can adeptly appraise and have an informed reading and understanding of the primary studies. That said, in our experience with our students, when working in a team of researchers/meta-analysts, it is not necessary that all members of the team have a solid, prerequisite knowledge of qualitative methods. It is sufficient that this level of expertise is available to the team, so perhaps at least one member of the team with that knowledge is enough. Similarly, previous experience of conducting qualitative research may be an advantage, given that many analytic processes used in QMA are the same as those used in other forms of qualitative research. However, again it is not essential that all members of the research team have had previous experience with qualitative research.

Although we do not prescribe working in a team when conducting a QMA, we do recommend it. An exception here would be instances in which the meta-analyst has familiarity with and expertise in the area on which the QMA focuses as well as solid knowledge of qualitative methods. Indeed, one of the first QMAs in psychotherapy had a single author (Timulak, 2007). The size of the research team may depend on the amount of work anticipated, which may be related to the size of the sample and the volume of data to be extracted (see Chapter 3, this volume). Knowledge of the field in which the meta-analysts conduct the QMA can help when estimating the expected workload (e.g., having an idea of the number of published studies in a given area).

FORMULATING THE RESEARCH QUESTION

Qualitative meta-analysts, similar to any (qualitative) researchers, break down the research problem into specific questions about what needs to be focused on in a particular study. In our experience, having a simple research question allows the meta-analysts to sharpen the focus and decide clearly which findings from the primary (original) studies contain information pertinent to the QMA. For instance, in one of our first attempts at conducting a QMA, the research question was very straightforward: "In qualitative psychotherapy process studies of significant events, what kinds of impacts do clients identify as being helpful?" (Timulak, 2007, p. 312). Even a very complex area of investigation allows for relatively simple and clear questions. For example, in a QMA that examined significant-insight events, Timulak and McElvaney (2013) were able to bring together detailed, in-depth analyses from the primary studies, combining the events' session transcripts together with the clients' and therapists' independent recollections of those events in the postsession interviews with a simple research question: "What processes are reported in qualitative studies investigating insight events in psychotherapy?" (p. 135). When thinking about a question for a QMA, we draw on our knowledge of the relevant field and awareness of potential studies; we can also inspect the research questions in the primary studies.

Specific research questions guide the selection of studies for a QMA (see Chapter 3) and then the selection of relevant parts of the selected studies that become the data for the QMA (see Chapter 4). In general, the research questions are set at the start of the study and typically remain unchanged because they are the guiding principle for everything we do in the QMA. However, QMA has an advantage of being flexible while not losing its rigor. Thus, we may also have a sort of evolving research question or questions; for example, we may start with a specific research question, but our early inspection of the potentially relevant studies may lead us to tweak our original question. Collins and Levitt (2021) offered an interesting example of how this can happen. They initially wanted to study an intersection of sexual minority development and religious identity development; however, they discovered that all the relevant studies were located within one particular religion. Therefore, they narrowed their scope (and their research question) and studied the intersection of sexual minority development and religious identity development in the context of this particular religion. In this example, the available research led to the adjustment of the research questions. Similarly, when we set out to study clients' experiences of therapy and find that many studies also include the clients' experiences of life changes attributed to therapy, we can broaden the focus of the QMA and study not only how clients experience therapy while they are in it but also what they report on how their life changed after the therapy ended.

DESIGNING THE QUALITATIVE META-ANALYSIS

In the chapters that follow, we present individual steps in conducting a QMA. After establishing a need for a QMA and formulating research questions, which we discussed in previous sections of this chapter, we need to identify and select primary studies. We then need to appraise them; extract data from them (all of these steps are discussed in Chapter 3); analyze the data while applying credibility checks (which we discuss in Chapters 4 and 5); and, finally, present the results (we focus on this in Chapters 4 and 6). Although we present a general outline of steps that can be taken in a QMA, we stress that the process of conducting a QMA is flexible, potentially iterative, and evolving, as we have already suggested. This flexibility poses potential challenges if the meta-analysts want to share (publish) a protocol for a QMA before they undertake it.

PLANNING AND PREREGISTERING THE QUALITATIVE META-ANALYSIS

In the context of a strong emphasis on the transparency of the research process and adhering to the standards developed for RCTs, which are currently expected to be preregistered (examples of registries can be found at https://clinicaltrials.gov and https://www.isrctn.com), it has also become standard to preregister quantitative meta-analyses and systematic reviews. By extension, it is now expected that QMAs will also be preregistered. Indeed, many journals (including in our field, psychotherapy), when considering a QMA, may expect that the submitted QMA was preregistered and that its protocol is available for scrutiny by the reviewers and, subsequently, readers.

A well-recognized example of a registry of protocols of planned meta-analyses is an international database of prospectively registered systematic reviews: the International Prospective Register of Systematic Reviews, commonly known as PROSPERO (https://www.crd.york.ac.uk/prospero/). PROSPERO is an open-access database that not only preregisters QMAs (and other forms of systematic reviews) but also offers guidelines and a structure for doing so (see Exhibit 2.1). This allows the meta-analysts to comply with standards for systematic reviews, such as the Preferred Reporting Items for Systematic Reviews and Meta-Analyses (known by the acronym PRISMA; Moher et al., 2009; Rethlefsen et al., 2021), that are currently expected of a systematic review (and thus also a QMA) by many scientific journals. The structure can therefore be used as a resource in the planning stages of QMA because it forces the meta-analysts to ask themselves important questions that will guide their work. Some questions that must be considered include the following:

- What is the QMA's research question?
- What will be the inclusion and exclusion criteria for the primary studies?
- How will studies be located?
- How will the data be extracted from the primary studies?
- How they will be analyzed?

In the remaining chapters of this book, we detail the issues that need to be considered during the process of conducting a QMA. In Chapter 7, we provide a summary of useful considerations.

Although not all QMA studies in psychology fit easily with the PROSPERO structure (e.g., the database is geared toward requirements most relevant to studying an intervention), potential meta-analysts should consider using it, and we encourage preregistration of a QMA. If the meta-analyst decides not to preregister their QMA, a good rationale should be provided as to why (e.g., there is no imminent policy implication that the QMA may influence). PROSPERO and similar clinical trial registries were initially established to enhance transparency and to prevent underreporting or selective reporting of unfavorable implications for an intervention in the results of trials (here, systematic reviews) or to prevent goals shifting in a trial or review so an intervention was viewed more favorably. Although it is not yet that common in psychology to preregister QMAs, there are good examples in existence. For instance, Almeida et al. (2019) published their QMA of cancer patients' fear of cancer recurrence in *Clinical Psychology Review* (it was perhaps the first QMA published in that journal) and had their QMA preregistered in PROSPERO (https://www.crd.york.ac.uk/prospero/display_record.php?RecordID= 36688).

EXHIBIT 2.1. Examples of PROSPERO Requirements for Systematic Reviews and Specifically for QMAs

Examples of General and QMA-Specific PROSPERO Requirements

Examples of general requirements for systematic reviews:

- Review title
- Anticipated or actual start date
- Anticipated completion date
- Stage of review at time of this submission (cannot be at the data extraction stage)
- Funding sources/sponsors
- Conflicts of interest
- Review question
- Searches
- URL to search strategy
- Condition or domain being studied
- Participants/population
- Intervention(s)
- Types of studies to be included
- Outcomes
- Data extraction (selection and coding)
- Risk-of-bias (quality) assessment
- Strategy for data synthesis
- Type and method of review
- Reference and/or URL for published protocol
- Details of any existing review of the same topic by the same authors
- Current status of review

QMA-specific requirements:

- Review question: Provides examples of frameworks that can guide a review question (see Booth et al., 2019)
- Context: Criteria for selection of studies
- Risk-of-bias assessment: How trustworthiness will be established
- Data synthesis: The method of extraction and synthesis of the data (e.g., thematic synthesis)

Note. The information in this exhibit refers to guidance pertaining to qualitative reviews and qualitative meta-analyses (QMAs). Full guidance can be found at https://www.crd.york.ac.uk/PROSPERO/#aboutregpage. PROSPERO = International Prospective Register of Systematic Reviews. From *PROSPERO: International Prospective Register of Systematic Reviews*, by National Institute for Health Research, n.d. (https://www.crd.york.ac.uk/PROSPERO/#aboutregpage). Adapted with permission.

SUMMARY

In this chapter, we outlined the key motivations and reasons for undertaking a QMA. We also noted that it is essential for the meta-analyst to have a robust knowledge of the field and an awareness of relevant research problems that a QMA could appropriately address. We also described considerations in the planning of a QMA and preregistering the study.

3

SELECTING AND APPRAISING PRIMARY STUDIES AND EXTRACTING THE DATA

In this chapter, we explain how to start answering a research question or questions by first identifying (all) relevant primary studies. We then discuss how to start the initial steps of data analysis by appraising the studies and highlighting the parts of those studies that contain the data relevant to the qualitative meta-analysis (QMA). We begin with the selection of studies. The process of selecting the studies we want to meta-analyze is equivalent to data collection in a regular (qualitative) research study. It is therefore a process central to any QMA.

SELECTION OF STUDIES

The research questions guide the development of the criteria for selecting the relevant studies. First, the research questions need to be transformed into key words, which are then used in the search engines of various databases. The key words may need to be further tweaked as the meta-analysts start to inspect the studies, but identifying relevant key words is the starting point. Given that a QMA is a form of systematic review, we recommend following

https://doi.org/10.1037/0000313-003
Essentials of Qualitative Meta-Analysis, by L. Timulak and M. Creaner

guidelines from the Preferred Reporting Items for Systematic Reviews and Meta-Analyses (PRISMA; Moher et al., 2009; Rethlefsen et al., 2021), which offers scaffolding for how to go about, report, and document the search.

The delineation of key words for initial searches is often complex. For instance, various databases maintain index terms—a *controlled vocabulary*— that may be a resource for selecting key words (e.g., Medline and PubMed use Medical Subject Headings, or MeSH, terms; see https://www.nlm.nih.gov/mesh/meshhome.html). By way of example, the American Psychological Association databases (e.g., PsycInfo) index their records with reference to the *Thesaurus of Psychological Index Terms* (see https://www.apa.org/pubs/databases/training/thesaurus), which is a set of standardized words for psychological concepts. Databases may also provide classification codes for specific subject matter that allow for the retrieval of articles within a particular subject category (e.g., "Psychotherapy & Psychotherapeutic Counseling" in PsycInfo). Boolean operators (AND, OR, NOT) may then be applied to expand or narrow a search (see Exhibit 3.1 for an example).

Meta-analysts need to ensure that the Boolean search and the key words being used are targeting pertinent studies. For instance, in Marren et al.'s (2022) QMA of clients' experiences of being in emotion-focused therapy (EFT; an older term for this therapy is *process–experiential*), we wanted to look at helpful, difficult-but-helpful, and unhelpful aspects identified by EFT clients. We were aware of a few EFT studies that have used Elliott's (1999) Client Change Interview schedule for data collection. That interview schedule asks questions across the domains (helpful, difficult-but-helpful, and unhelpful) that neatly fitted our research questions. We therefore wanted to see whether using the following Boolean search (i.e., qualitative OR "mixed method") AND ("emotion focused therapy" OR "emotion-focused therapy" OR "process

EXHIBIT 3.1. An Example of a Boolean Search From a Meta-Analysis on Clients' Experiences of Couples Therapy

1 Couple therapy / Marriage therapy / Marital therapy / Couple couns* / Marriage couns*
2 Client experience / Perception / Reflection / Therapeutic experience / Perspective / Helpful unhelpful aspect
3 Qualitative / Mixed method / Grounded theory / Thematic analysis / Content analysis/ Case study / Phenomenol* / Ethnograph* / Discourse analysis / Interpretative phenomenological analysis
4 1 + 2 + 3

Note. The asterisk used in a Boolean search denotes a truncated part of a word, for example "couns*." In this example, all words starting with the letters "couns" should be returned in the search. From *It Takes Three to Tango: Client's Experiences of Couple Therapy: A Meta-Analysis of Qualitative Research Studies* [Unpublished doctoral dissertation] (p. 91), by L. Madden, 2021. Copyright 2021 by L. Madden. Reprinted with permission.

experiential therapy" OR "process-experiential therapy" OR "EFT") AND ("client experience") would pick up the studies (that used the Client Change Interview schedule) we knew about and anticipated would end up in our final selection. We searched abstracts of several databases (e.g., PsycInfo, Web of Science). Given that we were able to locate relevant studies, we had increased confidence in our use of those key words in our search.

In a typical QMA, several databases may need to be searched, in particular in the context of multidisciplinary research (Harari et al., 2020). The databases relevant to psychology include PsycInfo, PubMed, Scopus, Web of Science, and so on. The meta-analysts may wish to consult a subject librarian as well (Sandelowski & Barroso, 2006). Each database may offer different options on how to conduct the search (e.g., the key words are used to search in platform-specific field codes, full texts vs. abstracts, or among the key words only; see Rethlefsen et al., 2021). The decisions on how to conduct the search can have significant implications in regard to the sheer volume of the studies the meta-analysts will need to scrutinize later given that some of the decisions (e.g., having very broad key words) may increase the volume of the studies that will need to be inspected for the inclusion into, or exclusion from, the QMA.

The key words that guide the selection of studies are further supplemented by other inclusion and exclusion criteria. These may involve methodological criteria, if there is a reason for the types of studies the meta-analysts want to include (e.g., any qualitative study pertaining to the research question or only studies that used certain types of narrowly defined methodology [e.g., only grounded theory studies]). We argue that there are significant similarities among qualitative methods, so we suggest including studies that used a range of qualitative methods (e.g., grounded theory, interpretative phenomenological analysis, consensual qualitative research). The meta-analysts can always examine whether the use of a specific brand name qualitative method had any impact on the type of findings generated by the studies (see the Appraisal of Primary Studies section). There may, however, be qualitative methods that the meta-analysts decide not to include because their methods are too divergent with the main body of primary studies generated and thus cannot easily be aggregated with them (e.g., communication-based approaches such as conversation analysis).

Similarly, the meta-analysts need to decide whether to include qualitative sections of mixed-methods studies. In our experience with psychotherapy research, including mixed-methods studies is a viable option. In such cases, the meta-analysts can predefine which parts of the mixed-methods studies are acceptable and relevant to their QMA. For instance, in QMAs that examined client-reported impacts in significant events, we accepted only the parts of the studies that did not use any predetermined category system (a taxonomy) to classify reported impacts (e.g., Ladmanová et al., 2021). Therefore, parts of studies that led to the generation of a category system could be acceptable because they were qualitative in nature, whereas the parts that involved the use of a developed category system (e.g., following percentages of certain types of impacts in different types of therapies) were not included because they would be considered quantitative (i.e., assigning frequencies into a nominal scale).

Decisions also need to be made about the time frame and range of years on which the QMA will focus. Meta-analysts typically seek to include all available studies, so they may be limited only by the age range included in the databases they search. Other times, meta-analysts may want to limit the publication dates because, for example, they may want to look at updating a previous QMA.

Furthermore, the inclusion and exclusion criteria can also apply limiters to the language of the original studies (it must be a language in which the meta-analysts are proficient). The criteria may also involve a decision on whether the meta-analysts will include only published studies or whether unpublished dissertations or other forms of materials (e.g., unpublished manuscripts) will also be included. Obviously, the latter are usually not accessible in the common databases that the meta-analysts peruse when selecting studies and may thus be accessed by searching the reference lists of the studies already located (or by seeing conference presentations or following a particular researcher's output and contacting them directly). The inclusion criteria may also include a required methodological standard that would be acceptable (see the Appraisal of Primary Studies section), such as a requirement that the studies were subject to a peer review process (Timulak, 2009).

As is the case with the evolving research questions—recall our discussion in Chapter 2—there may be flexibility in the development of the inclusion and exclusion criteria of a QMA. If this is the case, however, it needs to be well documented and declared to readers. In our experience, we do not typically change our original search terms for locating relevant papers. However, we may come across studies that our search identified but, on closer inspection, transpire to be a poor match for our inclusion criteria; consequently, we may further tweak our exclusion criteria. For instance, in Marren et al.'s (2022) QMA of clients' experiences of EFT we found that some researchers had used an integrative form of EFT whereby EFT was combined with some other therapy (e.g., cognitive behavior therapy). We had not anticipated this possibility, and thus we had to decide what to do with such studies. We consequently decided to update our exclusion criteria and exclude such studies.

Several systems can help meta-analysts to become cognizant of what to consider when deciding on the inclusion and exclusion criteria. The International Prospective Register of Systematic Reviews database (PROSPERO) suggests consulting two systems: (a) SPIDER (Sample–Phenomenon of Interest–Design–Evaluation–Research Type; Cooke et al., 2012; see also Booth, 2016) and (b) PICO (Population, Intervention, Comparison, Outcome; Centre for Reviews and Dissemination, 2009) when developing the Boolean search strategy (for a comparison of these, see Methley et al., 2014). These systems give examples of what needs to be considered; PICO in particular is intended for any (primarily quantitative) systematic review, whereas SPIDER is specifically intended for qualitative research.

The actual selection of studies is also a process. Eventually, the flow of the study selection is expected (by journals) to be captured in a PRISMA flow diagram (for an example, see Figure 3.1). The process typically starts with reviewing abstracts of the studies that were identified by the search key words. The studies that potentially meet the eligibility criteria may be selected at this stage. The meta-analysts also scrutinize duplications; that is, when the same study is picked up twice by the search. Sometimes duplication may occur because of the use of several databases, but at times the same database may generate a duplication. Eventually, the full texts are examined. This needs to include examination of the method (whether the study contains the required qualitative methodology) and the findings (whether the study may contribute to the focus of the QMA). At this stage, further duplications may be discovered, if single qualitative studies are reported across several papers. In such instances, the studies working off the same data set are usually combined into one record and treated as one study (Timulak, 2014).

Examination of abstracts, duplications, and full texts for the inclusion of the studies may be enhanced by the use of a software program (for a discussion of software options for systematic reviews, see Harrison et al., 2020). We have experience using Zotero (https://www.zotero.org) and find it very convenient because it allows the user to export the results of the various database searches. Furthermore, it allows for linking of the short-listed abstracts to the full texts for further scrutiny. Software solutions allow for expedient tracking of the various stages of study selection and may be a useful resource when preparing a PRISMA diagram.

The engine searches may need to be supplemented by hand searches. The references of the primary studies selected can be inspected; they may identify further relevant studies that were missed in the electronic search.

FIGURE 3.1. An Example PRISMA Flow Diagram

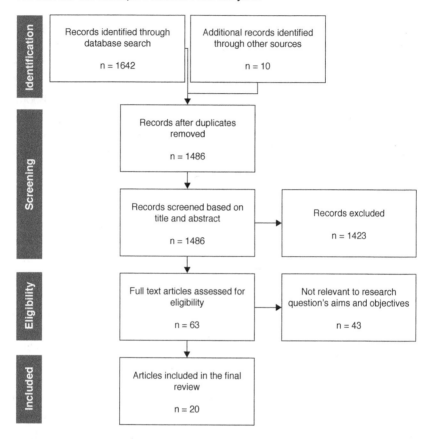

Note. PRISMA = Preferred Reporting Items for Systematic Reviews and Meta-Analyses (Moher et al., 2009). From *It Takes Three to Tango: Client's Experiences of Couple Therapy: A Meta-Analysis of Qualitative Research Studies* (p. 36) [Unpublished doctoral dissertation], by L. Madden, 2021. Copyright 2021 by L. Madden. Reprinted with permission.

The meta-analysts can also inspect specific and special issues of the journals that specialize in the topic of their QMA. Further tips for searching for qualitative studies that may potentially make it into the final QMA selection can be found in Booth (2016) and Finfgeld-Connett and Johnson (2013).

Another issue that meta-analysts need to consider, in particular if they do locate a significant number of primary qualitative studies that have examined a particular phenomenon, is whether they want to limit the number of studies that would contribute to the QMA. As with any systematic review, the selection of studies for a QMA is typically systematic, with an attempt to capture all relevant studies that will allow the meta-analysts to answer the question or questions posed by the specific QMA. We say "typically" because, as we have noted in our writing (i.e., Timulak & Creaner, in press), some QMA methodologists (e.g., Collins & Levitt, 2021) have suggested that the QMA may achieve a saturation point at which the QMA results appear to be stable (e.g., no new metacategories, no new findings are appearing) while the analysis is still progressing. At that point, some would argue that the meta-analysts could stop their analysis without evaluating all relevant studies. In such a case, the saturation is still preceded by the selection of all relevant studies, although not all contribute to the results.

Although we are saying that this is hypothetically possible, we are not aware of an example from psychology or a related field that would illustrate this point. In general, meta-analysts select and then analyze all identified studies that meet their inclusion/exclusion criteria. We are aware of just one example that first analyzed only a selection of potential studies, but even in this case the meta-analysis was then supplemented by additional analysis of the remaining identified studies. This example is a QMA by Levitt et al. (2016), who meta-analyzed 109 studies on clients' experiences of individual therapy. However, they initially conducted the meta-analysis by generating bottom-up meta-categories of only 67 studies they had located with various forms of searches. Once they had achieved saturation of their metacategories (i.e., the new studies were not bringing additional findings or metacategories), they converted the results into a taxonomy that was applied to the remainder of the studies they had located through conventional searches (the taxonomy in this case was used to assign the data to the already existing category system).

In contrast, we can also find examples of QMAs in which the selection of studies was limited by a very specific criterion. For instance, meta-analysts may combine the studies they have conducted or compare the results of specific studies. The search for all relevant studies is then quite limited, and the meta-analysts make a case for how their research problem or question is best answered by their specific search or selection strategy. The studies included in the QMA are then not really all of the potentially relevant studies available but the specific studies that the meta-analysts know about and want to examine in a combined analysis (a meta-analysis). An example of such a QMA is the work of Jennings et al. (2008), who meta-analyzed two studies they had conducted that used the same method, one an examination of master therapists in the United States and another one that focused on master therapists in Singapore. This type of QMA is not typical, but, apart from the study selection process, all other suggestions described in this book fit this type of QMA as well.

APPRAISAL OF PRIMARY STUDIES

The study selection process is closely aligned with the process of appraisal (i.e., assessment, evaluation) of the selected studies. Indeed, the appraisal of the primary studies may overlap with the final selection of QMA studies given that the quality of the methodology may be one of the inclusion criteria. For instance, QMAs often use an established appraisal system, such as the Critical Appraisal Skills Programme (CASP) Qualitative Research Checklist (2018; see Exhibit 3.2 and https://casp-uk.net/wp-content/uploads/2018/01/CASP-Qualitative-Checklist-2018.pdf). The CASP assesses the quality of a study on the basis of 10 criteria. The meta-analysts can pre-set a requirement for studies to be included in their QMA by stipulating that a study needs to meet at least seven of the 10 criteria. The meta-analysts are welcome to develop their own appraisal tool, but there now exists a number of tools that they may wish to consult (for a review of existing qualitative research appraisal tools specifically suitable to QMA, see Majid & Vanstone, 2018).

It is important to note, however, that the appraisal process goes beyond stipulations such as the ones suggested by the CASP checklist. An intrinsic part of a QMA is to establish how the phenomenon that is the focus of a QMA was examined in the primary studies. Hence, the appraisal of the primary studies not only serves the purpose of potentially selecting the studies but also is a part of the actual analysis given that the QMA involves finding out not only what the primary studies found but also how they came to their findings. For that purpose, the meta-analysts need first to identify the parts of the original primary studies that pertain to their research question because these will become the data for the QMA (see the Data Extraction

EXHIBIT 3.2. Examples of Critical Appraisal Skills Programme (CASP) Criteria

Examples of CASP Qualitative Research Checklist Criteria

- Was there a clear statement of the aims of the research?
- Was the research design appropriate to address the aims of the research?
- Were the data collected in a way that addressed the research issue?
- Was the data analysis sufficiently rigorous?

Note. From *CASP Checklist: 10 Questions to Help You Make Sense of a Qualitative Research* (pp. 2–5), by Critical Appraisal Skills Programme, 2018 (https://casp-uk.b-cdn.net/wp-content/uploads/2018/03/CASP-Qualitative-Checklist-2018_fillable_form.pdf). CC BY-NC-SA 3.0.

section), and they want to know about the characteristics of the relevant studies, such as the sample characteristics, data collection methods, data analysis methods, theoretical background of the researchers, and any unique features that may have affected the results. This initial mapping of the studies' characteristics typically finds its way to the final outline of the QMA in the form of a table (see Table 3.1, which presents examples of study characteristics from a QMA of client reports of helpful and unhelpful aspects of eating disorder treatment; Timulak et al., 2013).

One important characteristic of the appraisal process is that it is similar to the overall process of conducting a QMA, meaning it is flexible and iterative. For instance, the meta-analysts can discover late in a QMA that some feature of the data collection in the primary studies may have had an impact on what was reported and would then need to go back and review all the primary studies to see whether that feature was reported. This can also happen when a QMA paper is being evaluated in the peer review process for a journal. For instance, we and some of our colleagues were questioned by an anonymous reviewer as to whether we had missed a particular subset of studies in a QMA of client-reported helpful and unhelpful impacts in significant-events studies (Ladmanová et al., 2021). We had to go back and review the reasons why we did not include certain studies. It transpired that those studies did not report on the client-reported impacts in an open-ended manner because they had preselected events on the basis of a specific impact (e.g., insight). Thus, we had rightly not included them in the QMA because we wanted to look at the studies that had generated a variety of impacts (not just a specific impact). In any case, the review process triggered a reappraisal of already-selected studies.

DATA EXTRACTION

In essence, the main point of selecting the primary studies is to obtain relevant data for a QMA. The data for a QMA are typically located in the Results sections of the primary studies that pertain to the research questions the QMA is trying to answer. Given that the primary studies are qualitative studies (observational or interview-based research or their combination), their findings may be presented in the form of narratives, categories, themes, quotes from participants, and so on. On occasion, meta-analysts may need to examine the Discussion sections of the primary studies because they may contain quotes from participants or other findings that are still part of the results of the primary study. Given that the focus of a selected primary study may overlap only partly

TABLE 3.1. Examples of Methodological Characteristics of the Primary Studies From Timulak et al.'s (2013) Quantitative Meta-Analysis

Study	N	Sample	Therapy type	Data collection method	Data analysis method	Important methodological factors influencing results
Banasiak et al. (2007)	36 clients	BN: All Mean age = 29.5 Gender: Female This refers to the whole sample (n = 54), from which the subsample was studied. Participants were recruited from the community via newspaper advertisements; media announcements; and posters placed in GP waiting rooms, libraries, and community centers. Referrals also were made from a community-based ED information center.	Guided self-help (GSH), whereby a patient works through a CBT self-help manual guided by GP. There were nine treatment sessions of 20-30 minutes where support was provided by the GP working through the manual over a 16-week period.	Data were collected from a questionnaire: Treatment evaluation. Relevant open-ended questions: (1) What were (a) the most effective aspects of the GSH treatment approach and (b) the least effective aspects of the GSH treatment approach? (2) What were (a) the most helpful aspects of working with the GP and (b) the least helpful aspects of working with the GP?	Responses to each of the three questions were collated and subjected to a content analysis. Two authors independently reviewed responses, and meaningful response categories were generated through discussion. The assignment of responses to categories was performed by two independent raters who achieved an interrater reliability of .98. Differences in coded responses were discussed and resolved through a consensus.	The division of categories into subgroups is derived from the questionnaire. This is a "customer satisfaction survey" or "treatment evaluation" type of study.

| Button and Warren (2001) | 36 clients | AN: All Mean age = 27.9 Gender: Female Participants were from a cohort (83 females, 6 males) who had presented for treatment 7.5 years ago. Former patients (*n* = 79) were contacted in writing by the consultant psychiatrist to inquire about their willingness to participate in the study. | A specialist service for the treatment of adults with ED. It was broadly psychotherapeutic in nature, but medical interventions were also applied. | A semistructured interview (which took up to 2 hr) was used that also included administration of diagnostic questionnaires. The relevant part of the interview comprised two parts: their views of (a) the disorder and (b) the treatment. Several questionnaires were used with a relatively large original sample size, so this was a mixed-methods study. Most interviews were carried out in a hospital (*n* = 26), and 10 were interviewed in their home. | Methods of analysis are not described except for common themes identified during the interviews by direct quotes from individual subjects. | The study described how people live with ED, 7.5 years after their initial contact with a specialist for treatment. Relevant focus was: to further understand how the sufferer views the disorder and how they experienced treatment and help. Only text pertinent to this focus was coded. Authors offer common themes identified by direct quotes from individual subjects. The study is limited by the possibility that they may have selected quotes that back up the authors' perspective. |

(continues)

TABLE 3.1. Examples of Methodological Characteristics of the Primary Studies From Timulak et al.'s (2013) Quantitative Meta-Analysis (*Continued*)

Study	N	Sample	Therapy type	Data collection method	Data analysis method	Important methodological factors influencing results
Cockell et al. (2004)	32 clients	21 AN, 11 EDNOS, nine of whom were at subthreshold for AN. Mean age (of entire sample) = 27.9 Gender: Female Participants were those consecutively admitted to a 15-week residential ED treatment program. Women consecutively admitted to a residential program were invited to participate.	Details of the program are not given (i.e., specific treatments, psychological theories, etc., are missing). It was residential, lasting 15 weeks.	In-depth interviews were conducted.	A grounded theory approach, which involves a systematic process of indexing, coding, categorizing, and writing, was used to analyze the data. As data collection progressed, more detailed questions were asked, and reflections made to validate response and understanding.	Focus on maintenance of therapeutic change following ED treatment (i.e., identify factors that help or hinder the maintenance of change during the 6 months immediately following ED treatment). Not specifically focused on helpful and nonhelpful aspects of psychological therapy.

Note. BN = bulimia nervosa; CBT = cognitive behavior therapy; GP = general practitioner; AN = anorexia nervosa; ED = eating disorder; EDNOS = eating disorder not otherwise specified. From *Helpful and Unhelpful Aspects of Eating Disorders Treatment Involving Psychological Therapy: A Meta-Synthesis of Qualitative Research Studies* (pp. 19–20), by L. Timulak, J. Buckroyd, J. Klimas, M. Creaner, D. Wellsted, F. Bunn, S. Bradshaw, and G. Green, 2013, British Association for Counselling and Psychotherapy (https://www.bacp.co.uk/media/1980/bacp-helpful-unhelpful-aspects-eating-disorders-treatment-involving-psychological-therapies.pdf). Copyright 2013 by British Association for Counselling and Psychotherapy. Adapted with permission.

with the QMA's focus, the meta-analysts need to highlight only the parts of the primary study's results that pertain to the QMA's question (simple colored highlighting can be used).

For example, a QMA one of us was involved in (Marren et al., 2022) looked at clients' experiences of undergoing EFT. A selected primary study (O'Connell Kent et al., 2020) had examined the effectiveness of EFT for treatment of generalized anxiety symptoms in a university student population. This was a pre–post quantitative study, but it also included the clients' reports (in a posttherapy interview) of their experiences of undergoing EFT. For our QMA, we thus highlighted only the parts of that study that included the clients' reports on their experiences of helpful and unhelpful aspects of therapy. We excluded all quantitative results as well as qualitative results that did not refer to client experiences of helpful and unhelpful aspects of EFT (e.g., posttherapy client-reported changes). These relevant results from this primary study were presented in a table that listed categories of client experiences of helpful and unhelpful aspects of EFT and in a narrative that contained categories of clients' experiences with their brief description as well as client quotes illustrating those categories.

Localization and extraction of the data (i.e., the findings from the primary studies) for further analysis can be done hand in hand with highlighting (for which a different color can be used) of any part of the primary studies that contains information on the study characteristics relevant to the QMA. The data extraction process is also linked to the study selection and the appraisal of studies. These processes overlap sequentially. For instance, the meta-analysts can short-list (preliminarily select) a potential primary study because they scanned its Method section and expect that it used the method that is a part of our inclusion criteria (e.g., a qualitative study on the clients' experiences of EFT). They can then scan the Results section of the primary study to see whether it indeed contains the findings that can become the data for our further analysis. Once the potential study has been short listed, the meta-analysts can inspect it in detail and highlight all relevant study characteristics as well as all parts that can constitute the actual data for the meta-analysis.

Furthermore, regarding the identification of the data, the use of the original data set is sometimes mentioned in the research literature. In QMAs the meta-analysts normally include only the published findings and do not ask the authors for their original data sets. However, they can find suggestions for working with the original data sets in the literature (McCormick et al., 2003). We are not aware of studies that have used this approach in psychology or psychotherapy (with the exception of a very recent QMA wherein a research team cross-case analyzed eight case studies to which they had direct access because it comprised their cumulative data set; see Stephen et al., 2021). However, with the emphasis on open science and data sharing, the possibility of aggregating the original data sets is growing. In the context of qualitative research, this may pose ethical questions because the qualitative data may often render participants or contexts potentially identifiable (e.g., audio or video recordings or identifiable quotes; we discuss this further in Chapter 5).

SUMMARY

Meta-analysts have myriad decisions to make in terms of selecting the relevant studies and the parts of these studies that pertain to the QMA. In this context, we note the necessity of scrupulously recording and transparently reporting all of the decisions made throughout a QMA and their inherent rationale.

4 ANALYZING META-ANALYTIC DATA

After we select the studies for a qualitative meta-analysis (QMA) and highlight the data within them that pertain to the guiding research question or questions, we can start to work on our analyses of the identified data. The data analysis process starts with the delineation of a conceptual framework (comprising the domains of investigation) that organizes our data. The process of organizing data is influenced by our research question and the phenomenon under investigation. It is supplemented by the preparation of the data and with the categorization, or clustering, of the data. In this chapter, we take readers through the data analysis process, discussing important aspects of this stage of the QMA, such as credibility checks, presentation of findings, and the examination of the influence of the methods in the original studies on the findings of the QMA.

Although we say that the data analysis process starts with the delineation of a conceptual framework that organizes data, we begin here by discussing the data preparation step because it is closely linked to the data localization and extraction. In reality, the process of conducting a QMA is, as we have mentioned, flexible and iterative, so, for instance, although the research questions guide our conceptual framework for what constitutes the data

https://doi.org/10.1037/0000313-004
Essentials of Qualitative Meta-Analysis, by L. Timulak and M. Creaner

(i.e., which findings from the primary studies are relevant for the QMA), the inspection of the data may also refine the conceptual framework.

DATA PREPARATION

After we highlight all available data pertaining to the research question, we start to organize them to manageable chunks. The term we use for the delineation of a manageable chunk of data is a *meaning unit* (MU; originally used by Giorgi, 1985, and by Rennie et al., 1988, but our use of the term is more aligned with that used by Elliott & Timulak, 2021). The MU is the smallest piece of data (unit) that can stand on its own and enable the reader to determine its meaning. To develop a MU, we simply take the highlighted parts of the primary studies and break them into small units that deliver a meaning on their own. This process is arbitrary, and every meta-analyst may have their own style and approach. In a regular qualitative study (not a meta-analysis), there are a few options for how to approach this. We can break the text (transcribed interviews or observations) into units spanning from a sentence to a short paragraph that is conveying a meaning (i.e., is understood on its own without the need to read the text before the unit and the text after it). As detailed by Elliott and Timulak (2021), a MU may convey more than one meaning because the text may have a layered meaning, in particular if it is a bigger MU. This is not a major problem because the later analysis allows for a MU to be considered multiple times when trying to generate clusters of MUs of similar meanings (see the Generating Metacategories section).

The relevant parts of the text from the primary studies, as highlighted in the previous step (locating and extracting the data; see Chapter 3, this volume), come in varied forms. The data may be present in the form of a table containing the findings of the primary study reported as categories or themes; the data may be present in the form of a description of the categories or themes, or they may be present in the form of a narrative or as quotes from the participants. Often, all these possibilities are present within one study. Thus, we naturally start to have MUs that may vary dramatically in format. For example, in Marren et al.'s (2022) QMA of clients' experiences of helpful and unhelpful aspects of therapy, when analyzing a primary study conducted by O'Connell Kent et al. (2020) that we mentioned at the end of Chapter 3 (see the Data Extraction section in that chapter), we can have MUs that capture helpful aspects of therapy, ranging from categories taken from a table, such as "Chair/ experiential work [was helpful]" (for readers unfamiliar with psychotherapy, *chair work* refers to a standard practice of emotion-focused therapy [EFT] that uses imaginary/experiential dialogues) to quotes of varying length, such as

> I felt that [my therapist] actually did kind of care about my progress and she seemed really happy for me if there was stuff going well and like that made a big, big difference because eh, it felt like she wasn't just like a job for her if you know what I mean? (The quote has been slightly shortened.)

As we are breaking down the relevant data from the primary studies into manageable MUs, we are also assigning them *meaning unit ID tags*, so we can trace them in all steps of our analysis (Elliott & Timulak, 2021). The tags are simple and efficient reference points for the later analysis, auditing, or other activities focused on building the credibility of a QMA. Some meta-analysts may prefer to develop their own tagging system. We (Timulak & Creaner, in press) recommend referencing the first author of the primary study, year of publication, and a number that we would assign to a MU (starting from 1 and continuing indefinitely). Thus, the MU "Chair/experiential work [was helpful]" could get the tag *O'Connell Kent/2020/MU1*, and the following quote—

> I felt that [my therapist] actually did kind of care about my progress and she seemed really happy for me if there was stuff going well and like that made a big, big difference because eh, it felt like she wasn't just like a job for her if you know what I mean?

—could get the tag *O'Connell Kent/2020/MU2*.

CONCEPTUAL FRAMEWORK ORGANIZING THE DATA: DOMAINS OF INVESTIGATION

As we previously noted, and we think it important to reiterate, any data analysis in a qualitative study, including a QMA, is shaped by the research question and the nature of the investigated phenomenon. The research question shapes our domains of investigations (Elliott & Timulak, 2021; Timulak & Elliott, 2019). In a single qualitative study, the domains of investigation can be further defined by how the data are collected (e.g., through an interview schedule that offers a structure through which the researchers approach the phenomenon) or how they were influenced by the nature of the phenomenon (e.g., the client's experience of therapy is shaped by their experiences of the therapist's actions in relation to the client's presentation). Domains of investigation can be also defined chronologically (e.g., what happened first, what happened then, and what happened after) or theoretically (e.g., what are the primary maladaptive emotions, as defined in EFT, that clients with depression present?). In reality, the domains of investigation can be shaped by a blend of these stated reasons or through other pragmatic consider- ations (e.g., what appears to be practical and accessible).

In a QMA, the domains of investigation are defined through similar pro- cesses and stem from the research problem or question. Delineation of a QMA's domain of investigation thus starts before we locate the primary studies and the data within them. For instance, we can be interested in clients' expe- riences of helpful and unhelpful aspects of EFT. Because we are researchers and theorists in that area of psychotherapy research, we know that there should be a number of (primary) studies that have investigated these types of clients' perspectives. We also know that at least some of the studies that should end up in our selection (because we are familiar with them) have used the Client Change Interview (see Chapter 3, p. 26, of Elliott, 1999) to collect information on this type of client experience. The Client Change Interview asks, among other things, about the clients' experiences of helpful aspects of therapy, difficult-but-helpful aspects of therapy, and unhelpful aspects of therapy. We can therefore decide before we begin our QMA that we will be interested in the clients' experiences of (a) helpful aspects of EFT, (b) difficult- but-helpful aspects of EFT, and (c) unhelpful aspects of EFT. These three aspects will essentially be our three research questions as well as our three domains of investigation that will organize data.

In the next step of our meta-analysis (see the Assigning Data to Domains of Investigation section), we assign all relevant data (eventually also broken into MUs) into the three domains of investigation (helpful, difficult-but- helpful, and unhelpful aspects of EFT). The two MUs that we used as examples earlier—*O'Connell Kent/2020/MU1* and *O'Connell Kent/2020/MU2*—both refer to helpful aspects of EFT and would thus be assigned to Domain 1: Helpful Aspects of EFT.

In this example, we decided on the domains of investigation before starting the QMA. However, as we continue to underscore, the whole process of a QMA is iterative and flexible, so if we discovered that it is too complicated to distinguish between the helpful and difficult-but-helpful aspects of EFT (e.g., because many of the primary studies did not use this distinction), we could collapse these two domains into one. Therefore, although we may set out to conduct a QMA with clear ideas about the domains of investigation, these may evolve as we start to interact with the data (i.e., when we start to locate and extract the data). Furthermore, in terms of the QMA process when we examine a number of studies, we may discover that the original domains of investigation are too broad, and we may thus divide them into subdomains. In a QMA investigating helpful and unhelpful aspects of eating disorder

(ED) treatment that involved psychological therapy, Timulak et al. (2013) decided to streamline the conceptual framework further and divided the two main domains—1: Helpful Aspects of Treatment and 2: Unhelpful Aspects of Treatment—into several subdomains. Table 4.1 presents an example of how the unhelpful aspects of treatment were further divided.

This process of dividing the domains of investigations into subdomains needs to be distinguished from a hierarchical organization of findings (that we refer to as *metacategories* here and that are presented in the next section). The division of domains into subdomains does not tell us yet what we found. For instance, in the example given in Table 4.1, the division of domains into subdomains simply tells us that unhelpful aspects of the treatment may pertain to the mental health professional or to general or specific characteristics of the treatment. It does not tell us exactly what the unhelpful aspects of the ED treatment are in these three subdomains (1: the mental health professional, 2: the general characteristics, and 3: the specific characteristics of the treatment), which would be the actual findings of the QMA.

It is also possible that a broadly defined research question (domain of investigation) is broken into more detailed subdomains after an initial inspection of the located and extracted data within the selected primary studies. Consider, for example, a QMA that examined processes in session recordings of significant events (together with the clients' and therapists' independent recall of those events) that led to insight as reported by the clients. The main research question in this QMA was quite broad: "What processes are reported in qualitative studies investigating insight events in psychotherapy?" (Timulak & McElvaney, 2013, p. 134). This domain of investigation was then broken into several subdomains that were linked together into a grid of nine (3 × 3;

TABLE 4.1. Domains of Investigation in Timulak et al.'s (2013) Quantitative Meta-Analysis: An Example of a Domain and Selected Subdomains

Domain of investigation	Selected subdomains
Unhelpful Aspects of Eating Disorder Treatment Involving Psychological Therapy	• Deficiencies in Important Characteristics of Mental Health Professional • Deficiencies in Important General Characteristics of Treatment • Deficiencies in Important Specific Characteristics of Treatment

Note. From *Helpful and Unhelpful Aspects of Eating Disorders Treatment Involving Psychological Therapy: A Meta-Synthesis of Qualitative Research Studies* (pp. 47–48), by L. Timulak, J. Buckroyd, J. Klimas, M. Creaner, D. Wellsted, F. Bunn, S. Bradshaw, and G. Green, 2013, British Association for Counselling and Psychotherapy (https://www.bacp.co.uk/media/1980/bacp-helpful-unhelpful-aspects-eating-disorders-treatment-involving-psychological-therapies.pdf). Copyright 2013 by British Association for Counselling and Psychotherapy. Adapted with permission.

see Table 4.2). Three domains were defined by who was the actor/reflector of the process (Client's Process, Therapist Process, and Client–Therapist Interaction) and three sequential domains (Context [i.e., what led into the event], Event and Key Intervention, and Impact [the consequences of the event]). This conceptual framework was delineated after the selected studies had been inspected because it was apparent that the primary studies in general used a variant of a similar framework that looked at the clients' and therapists' processes and their interaction in a clear chronological order.

Timulak and McElvaney's (2013) study is an example of a QMA in which the domain structure of the QMA was informed by the domain structure of the original primary studies. The domain structure of some primary studies can thus inform the overall conceptual framework (the domain structure) of the QMA. Timulak (2014) noted that there may be a particularly comprehensive primary study whose conceptual framework may be especially useful in conceptualizing the studied phenomenon and that can inform the framework eventually used by the QMA.

All of the examples of conceptual frameworks (domains of investigation) we have provided so far either involved combining the characteristics of the phenomena (e.g., therapy has two participants, a client and a therapist who are engaged in their own process and interact with each other) and a sequential (chronological) ordering of events (e.g., before or after the event), or they were domains defined by practical utility (e.g., what is helpful and unhelpful). Domains of investigation can, however, also be anchored in theory. Almeida et al. (2019) presented a QMA of patients diagnosed with cancer and their experiences of the fear of cancer recurrence. Their QMA data analysis was explicitly informed by the *emotion scheme* theoretical

TABLE 4.2. An Example of a Domains-of-Investigation Grid in a Significant-Insight Events Qualitative Meta-Analysis

	Client process (intent, expressed content, emotional experience, reflection)	Therapist process (intent, intervention, reflection/ observation)	Therapist and client interaction
Context (Lead-In to the Event)			
Event and Key Intervention			
Impact/Consequences			

Note. From "Qualitative Meta-Analysis of Insight Events in Psychotherapy," by L. Timulak and R. McElvaney, 2013, *Counselling Psychology Quarterly, 26*(2), pp. 11–12 (https://doi.org/10.1080/09515070.2013.792997). Copyright 2013 by Taylor & Francis Ltd. Adapted with permission.

framework that originated in EFT theory. Thus, they structured all the data from the primary studies into domains such as Experienced/Implicit Emotion (e.g., what emotions patients experience and express in reference to the recurrence of cancer), Perceptual–Situational (triggers; e.g., situations that elicit the fear-of-recurrence experiences), Symbolic–Conceptual (e.g., cognitions associated with the fear-of-recurrence experiences), Motivational–Behavioral (e.g., action tendencies contained in the fear-of-recurrence experiences), and Bodily–Expressive (e.g., bodily expression of the experienced emotions related to the fear of recurrence). The data located in and extracted from the selected primary studies were then allocated to these theoretically informed domains.

ASSIGNING DATA TO DOMAINS OF INVESTIGATION

So far, we have mentioned two steps of the data analysis: (a) data preparation (delineation of MUs) and (b) delineation of an organizing (conceptual) structure of the data (which we also call *domains of investigations*). Chronologically, these two steps are closely linked and can go in either order: We can either assign the located and extracted data (not yet broken into MUs) into the domains of investigation (that can be predetermined, or predetermined and further tweaked, or evolving after we start to inspect the data), or we can first *prepare* data (i.e., break down the raw located/extracted data into MUs) and then assign them to the domains of investigation that were present in some form from the start of the study (because they are guided by the research question). The exact sequence will depend on the specific study, but there is no problem if we start at any point in this sequence given that the process of conducting a QMA is flexible and iterative.

The conceptual framework (domains of investigation), though, implicitly precedes the localization/extraction and preparation of the data. Because we have domains of investigation formulated, we know what constitutes our data when we conduct the literature search (relevant primary studies selection). For the same reason, Elliott and Timulak (2021, pp. 42–44) explicitly put the domains of investigation sequentially before the data collection (in the QMA the order would be study selection and data localization/extraction) and data preparation. The actual analysis will then come with the generation of categories, which in QMA we call *metacategories* (see the Generating Metacategories section).

Before we look at the generation of categories, we want to stress again why it is important to talk about the domains of investigation. We highlighted the issue of delineating the domains in some of our earlier publications (Elliott & Timulak, 2021; Timulak & Elliott, 2019; Timulak & Creaner, in press). One of the typical problems in qualitative research in general (not specifically QMA) is that qualitative researchers conflate what they set out to study with what they find. For example, the researchers may want to study helpful aspects of therapy (a domain of investigation) and report that the main category (finding) is called "Helpful Aspects of Therapy." We see this conflation—of what the researchers set out to study with what they find— again and again in dissertations, in the papers we review, and, on occasion, in published qualitative studies. Perhaps it has to do with the early adaptation of grounded theory methodology in psychology and other disciplines. Because the grounded theory method encouraged researchers to conclude their analysis with one "core" category (the main finding) that would capture what would define all subcategories, it perhaps in some cases led to a level of abstraction that basically conflated the finding with the research questions (e.g., Research Question: What do clients report as helpful in therapy? Main Finding: Helpful aspects of therapy). We therefore urge meta-analysts to distinguish between their research question (which gets translated into domains of investigation) and the QMA findings that are answers to this question (metacategories).

GENERATING METACATEGORIES

Once we have assigned data to the delineated domains of investigation (eventually in the format of MUs), we start the analysis of the data (MUs) within the domains. Basically, at this stage we start to look at similarities across the MUs within the same domain and start to cluster MUs of similar meaning together. The term often used in qualitative research for this activity is *constant comparison* (of MUs; Glaser & Strauss, 1967). For instance, these two MUs in the domain of difficult-but-helpful aspects of EFT (both in a form of a category and a quote), which come from two different studies, can be clustered together:

> Twelve of thirteen participants described chair work specifically as difficult but helpful, as the quote from Niamh illustrates: [Laughs] "Despite my best efforts, it did help me separate—the chairs is what I'm talking about now, so uncomfortable, I fought against that a lot. Em, but it did help, I think it did fulfill its purpose"—*O'Connell Kent/2020/MU8*[1]

---

[1]The tag numbers are fictional.

Twelve clients referred to experiential work/depth of work as being difficult, but helpful (e.g., by the end I loved the chair work, but initially I found it hard). —*Timulak/2017/MU17*

Both MUs appear to capture the difficulty that clients are having with imaginary (experiential) dialogues (which are a defining part of EFT) but that clients still see value in them. The MUs can therefore be clustered together on the basis of similarity. Once we have several MUs coming from varied studies in a cluster, we can use a provisional name for that cluster (e.g., "Imaginary Dialogues Uncomfortable But Valued"). We at first discuss provisional categories, and, because the categorization (sorting and classifying) is happening in the context of a QMA, we use the term *metacategory* to distinguish them from categories that may be denoting findings in the primary studies. The metacategories thus become results/findings of the QMA.

We initially use provisional labels (which may be evolving as we progress with the constant comparison) for emerging metacategories, but once we have clustered all the QMA data (all the MUs) we settle on the final wording of all the metacategories. The name of each metacategory needs to not only capture the meaning contained in the MUs but also succinctly communicate to the reader the essence and meaning of a cluster of MUs (a metacategory). The actual name or title of a metacategory is crucial to the success of a QMA. We (Elliott & Timulak, 2021; Timulak & Elliott, 2019) have likened the development of metacategory names to crafting a poem and creating poetry. The metacategories' names have to be catchy and clear, evocatively and succinctly capturing the essence of what is trying to be conveyed. There optimally will be symmetry among the metacategories generated in a QMA. If, for example, the metacategories' names contain adjectives, they all should do so consistently. Similarly, if they consist of nouns only, or brief sentences, they should be in this format throughout. The symmetry should be present in the overall outline of the metacategories (see the Format of Metacategories/ Findings section).

The reading, clustering, and naming of MUs (categorizing) is an interpretive activity. At times, we have to rely solely on the primary study researchers' interpretation because a MU from an original study may contain no direct quote but only a categorization or narrative by the primary study researchers. A triple hermeneutic is thus at play (Weed, 2008) in that the primary researchers interpret the participants, and we interpret the primary researchers. At other times, we can make an assessment of the primary researchers' interpretation if we see a snippet of the raw data in an illustrative quote that supports the primary researcher's classification of the data (categorization) in the original study. If we see both the primary researchers' classification (e.g., a category or theme they created) and an illustrative quote from the participants (raw data), then we can, to a certain extent, assess the interpretive process of the primary study researchers. Both our examples above contain two elements: (a) a category (e.g., experiential work or depth of work is the category in the second quote given earlier [*Timulak/2017/MU17*]) and (b) an illustrative quote (e.g., "By the end I loved the chair work, but initially I found it hard"). The data are thus reasonably rich, and we as meta-analysts may be more confident that we understand more about the primary researchers' reading and interpretation of the data than if the primary study did not offer any quotes from the participants illustrating the category.

INTERPRETIVE LENS: SITUATING THE META-ANALYSTS

As we highlighted in the preceding section, the clustering, classification, and eventual labeling of similar MUs into metacategories is not only a descriptive but also an interpretive endeavor. For that reason, it is important that we can situate the interpretive framework of the primary researchers as well as our own as meta-analysts. Qualitative studies have a tradition of being open about the professional, personal, and theoretical background of the researchers. This is the type of information that we are collecting as a part of our appraisal of important study characteristics (see Chapter 3) and scrutinize further when we assess how these characteristics may have influenced the findings.

Although many qualitative methodologists (e.g., Fischer, 2009) stress the importance of not influencing the data and bracketing their own expectations, and we understand that it is about the rigor of the analysis and thoroughness of the researcher's work, we are skeptical about the extent to which bracketing is possible. Timulak and Elliott (2019) argued that the bracketing of one's own preconceptions, although a valuable activity, is possible only to a certain extent given that these preconceptions are ever present, and they shape how we read the data and how we report on our reading. For instance, the provisional metacategory created to capture our two MUs from the example given earlier (*O'Connell Kent/2020/MU8* and *Timulak/2017/MU17*)—"Imaginary Dialogues Uncomfortable But Valued"—was offered by the meta-analysts (for the purpose of this book, us [Laco and Mary]; we both have experiential therapy theoretical leanings). Furthermore, Laco happened to be involved in both primary studies in the example (although both contained a team of researchers with relatively broad theoretical orientations). Thus, our reading of and reporting on the data in the provisional metacategory label may acknowledge the clients' reported difficulties but also may emphasize clients' valuing of the imaginary dialogue interventions. Perhaps if the meta-analysts' team consisted purely of therapists/researchers of another orientation (e.g., cognitive therapists), the provisional label for the metacategory could read "Imaginary Dialogues Seen as Useful But Unnecessarily Uncomfortable." Thus, the meta-analysts' background (personal, professional, theoretical) is important and should be explicitly stated and reflected on in terms of whether and how it could have affected the meta-analysis.

One way of addressing the issue of the meta-analysts' situatedness and position when approaching data (the findings of primary studies) is to have an explicitly theoretically informed approach to the QMA (for a general discussion of theoretically informed qualitative research, see Hissa & Timulak, 2020). Here, the meta-analysts declare their theoretical framework for the reader to consult in more depth if they wish. The language that the meta-analysts then use in capturing their meta-analytic findings is clearly shaped by the explicitly acknowledged theoretical framework (e.g., Almeida et al., 2019, who used an emotion scheme theoretical framework; see also p. 40 of this book). For instance, when Almeida et al. (2019), in their motivational/ behavioral domain (that contains action tendencies contained in the fear-of-cancer-recurrence experiences), reported on

> experiential avoidance such as moving oneself away from experiences involving illness/treatment/death or avoidant self-related action tendencies such as trying not to think, or talk, or hear about cancer or about isolating oneself out not wanting people to feel sorry for the self,

we recognize the language of emotion scheme theory. The explicit theoretical situatedness of the meta-analysts allows the reader to clearly understand how the meta-analysts' background shaped their reading and analysis (classification) of the data and the format of the presentation of this analysis (the actual metacategories).

FORMAT OF METACATEGORIES/FINDINGS

When we talk about the findings of a QMA, we are referring to metacategories. We distinguish them from the domains of investigation that organize the data. We use the term *metacategory* for the findings of a QMA and the term *domains of investigation* for the sort of questions or areas of investigation that the findings populate. Some qualitative researchers may use the terms *domains of investigation* and *metacategories* differently (e.g., interchangeably), so we alert the reader to our use of these two words that distinguishes their respective function: (a) domain (area of investigation, e.g., helpful aspects of therapy) and (b) metacategory (a finding within some domain, e.g., being listened to by the therapist).

We often end up in our QMAs with a set of metacategories that can be further described in the main text of the QMA paper and presented in a table to facilitate the reader's understanding of the results. Table 4.3 contains an example of metacategories from an early QMA on helpful impacts reported by clients in significant-events studies (Timulak, 2007). The left column presents metacategories (in italics) and their brief definition and description, and the right column indicates which findings, and from which studies, fed into the metacategories (there were seven studies included in the meta-analysis). The table is in the original QMA article's Results section. It is supplemented by a narrative presentation of findings that included quotes taken from the primary studies illustrating each metacategory. For instance, the *Awareness–Insight–Self-Understanding* metacategory is illustrated by several quotes, among them these two: (a) "I realized I am desperate for support" (Moreno et al., 1995) and (b) "Understanding how I react to my husband like I do with my dad" (Cummings et al., 1993).

Metacategories can be also hierarchically structured into a higher order organization (i.e., superior metacategories that cover a cluster of metacategories according to some similarity in their meaning). We may decide to structure the metacategories into possible higher order metacategories when we have a lot of metacategories, which may be overwhelming for the reader. If we have a lot of metacategories, we may try to see if we could cluster metacategories on the basis of similarity into higher (second order) metacategories. Table 4.4 illustrates an example of a QMA (Timulak & Creaner, 2010) in which we meta-analyzed client-reported outcomes in person-centered/experiential psychotherapies. As one can see in the table, there are three main metacategories—(a) Appreciating Experiences of Self, (b) Appreciating Experience of Self in Relationship With Others, and (c) Changed View of Self/Others—that in themselves subsume 11 metacategories (Smoother and Healthier Emotional Experiencing; Appreciating Vulnerability; Experience of Self-Compassion, etc.).

The two examples (Tables 4.3 and 4.4) in which we show how QMA findings can be displayed offer also a flavor of findings from the original primary studies that fed into the metacategories (the far-right column in both tables). The sharing of the primary studies' findings in the main Results section of a published QMA may not be always possible because the number of primary studies may be much bigger than the seven and nine with which we worked in those early meta-analyses. Our current experience relates more

TABLE 4.3. Examples of Meta-Analytic Categories of Helpful Impacts and Corresponding Categories From Primary Studies

Meta-analytic categories of impacts	Categories of impacts in primary studies
Awareness-Insight-Self-Understanding: From different levels of becoming aware of the aspects of experience or broadly defined life situation (including others) to deeper contextual (including past influence) understanding of the experience or life situation	Evidence (in all seven studies): focusing awareness (Elliot, 1985), new focus (Wilcox-Matthew, Ottens, & Minor, 1997), new or different cognitive information about coping with problems (Heppner, Rosenberg, & Hedgespeth, 1992), problem clarification (Elliott, 1985), new perspective (Elliott, 1985), insight (Cummings, Slemon, & Hallberg, 1993), insight (Moreno, Fuhriman, & Hileman, 1995), insight (Timulak & Lietaer, 2001), insight (Wilcox-Matthew, Ottens, & Minor, 1997), awareness/insight (Timulak, Belicova, & Miler, 2003), clearer understanding (Timulak, Belicova, & Miler, 2003)
Behavioral Change-Problem Solution: As a result of the event the client possesses a new strategy to attain wished goals	Evidence (in four studies): problem solution (Elliott, 1985), identifying or experimenting with new ways of being (Cummings, Slemon, & Hallberg, 1993), new behavior (Wilcox-Matthew, Ottens, & Minor, 1997), what client is doing or will do differently in problem solving (Heppner, Rosenberg, & Hedgespeth, 1992)
Empowerment: The client experiences a fresh sense of personal strength to cope with problems, self-perceptions, interpersonal difficulties; the client has a sense of personal development; interpersonal validation may be present as well; also aspect of recognition of own development maybe present	Evidence (in three studies): empowerment (Timulak & Lietaer, 2001), empowerment (Timulak, Belicova, & Miler, 2003), empowerment after therapist's affirmation (Timulak & Lietaer, 2001; Timulak, Belicova, & Miler, 2003), self-satisfaction (Timulak & Lietaer, 2001), personal growth (Cummings, Slemon, & Hallberg, 1993)
Relief: Experiential relaxation due to the interpersonal experience of safety with the therapist or due to the less overwhelming experiencing of the concern where the therapist input (empathy, affirmation, hopefulness) may play role	Evidence (in three studies): relief (learning about therapy; Timulak, Belicova, & Miler, 2003), relaxation (due to seeing therapist concerned; Timulak & Lietaer, 2001), promotion of hope (Timulak, Belicova, & Miler, 2003), relief (feeling understood, affirmed; Timulak, Belicova, & Miler, 2003), reconciliation with unresolved issue (Timulak, Belicova, & Miler, 2003), concern attenuated (Wilcox-Matthew, Ottens, & Minor, 1997)

(continues)

TABLE 4.3. Examples of Meta-Analytic Categories of Helpful Impacts and Corresponding Categories From Primary Studies (*Continued*)

Meta-analytic categories of impacts	Categories of impacts in primary studies
Exploring Feelings–Emotional Experiencing: The client experiences emotions freshly, possibly in a new way, describes it as an important experience	Evidence (in four studies): emotional experience (Moreno, Fuhriman, & Hileman, 1995), exploring feelings (Cummings, Slemon, & Hallberg, 1993), being moved/vulnerable (Timulak & Lietaer, 2001), new or different experience (Heppner, Rosenberg, & Hedgespeth, 1992)
Feeling Understood: The (most) important aspect of the event was the client's feeling to be deeply understood, which brought a unique interpersonal experience	Evidence (in four studies): understanding (Elliott, 1985), understanding (Moreno, Fuhriman, & Hileman, 1995), empowerment/understanding (Timulak & Lietaer, 2001), exact naming (Timulak, Belicova, & Miler, 2003), feeling understood (Timulak, Belicova, & Miler, 2003)
Client Involvement: Event is significant because it makes the client actively participate in therapeutic process, because it contains space for the client to come up with what is important in his/her current judgment of therapeutic process	Evidence (in three studies): client involvement (Elliott, 1985), having influence on therapeutic process (Timulak & Lietaer, 2001), client glad that they could open up important theme (Timulak, Belicova, & Miler, 2003), delight from therapists' operations (Timulak & Lietaer, 2001)
Reassurance–Support–Safety: Includes accounts of client-experienced reassurance provided by the therapist with and without explicit verbal reassurance; it also contains experience of being accepted by the therapist and in the group format also identification with the other group members and experience of universality (the others experience the same or similar things)	Evidence (in all seven studies): assurance in therapeutic process (Timulak & Lietaer, 2001), assurance in therapist (Timulak & Lietaer, 2001; Timulak, Belicova, & Miler, 2003), good relationship (Cummings, Slemon, & Hallberg, 1993), reassurance (Elliott, 1985), emotional support (Heppner, Rosenberg, & Hedgespeth, 1992), being supported (Wilcox-Matthew, Ottens, & Minor, 1997), acceptance (Moreno, Fuhriman, & Hileman, 1995), identification (Moreno, Fuhriman, & Hileman, 1995), universality (Moreno, Fuhriman, & Hileman, 1995)
Personal Contact: Client experiences therapist not like a doctor but rather like a fellow human being; also experienced closeness may be present	Evidence (in three studies): personal contact (Elliott, 1985), personal contact (Timulak, Belicova, & Miler, 2003), relationship (Moreno, Fuhriman, & Hileman, 1995)

Note. The citations in this table are in the original table, and readers who are interested in any of the cited articles may consult Timulak (2007). From "Identifying Core Categories of Client Identified Impact of Helpful Events in Psychotherapy: A Qualitative Meta-Analysis," by L. Timulak, 2007, *Psychotherapy Research, 17*(3), p. 315 (https://doi.org/10.1080/10503300600608116). Copyright 2007 by Taylor & Francis Ltd. Adapted with permission.

TABLE 4.4. Example of Hierarchically Structured Metacategories of Client-Reported Outcomes in Person-Centered/Experiential Therapies

Main metacategory	Metacategories	Primary studies' findings
Appreciating Experiences of Self	Smoother and Healthier Emotional Experiencing	Hopefulness (Klein & Elliott, 2006), peace and stability (Klein & Elliott, 2006), emotional well-being, greater sense of energy (Klein & Elliott, 2006); calmer, at peace (Elliott, 2002a; Lipkin, 1954); improved mood, optimism (Elliott et al., 1990); general openness to own feelings (Elliott et al., 1990); ability to express and contain feelings (Dale et al., 1998); feeling more free and easy, more light and lively (Lipkin, 1954; 4/8; three out of eight studies on individual therapy)
	Appreciating Vulnerability	Permission to feel the pain (Rodgers, 2002); transparency (dropping barriers and defenses; Rodgers, 2002); honest with self (Rodgers, 2002; Elliott, 2002a); open to change (Elliott, 2002); awareness of being old, process of grieving, grieving is undoing problematic anger/anxiety (Elliott, 2002); self-acceptance of existential isolation (Dale et al., 1998); more tolerant of difficulties and setbacks (Elliott et al., 2009; 4/8)
	Experience of Self-Compassion	Self-esteem, self-care (Klein & Elliott, 2006), improved self-esteem (Elliott et al., 1990); engagement with self (experiencing support from within; Rodgers, 2002); valuing self (Dale et al., 1998; 4/8)
	Experience of Resilience	Restructuring (recycling the bad things; Rodgers, 2002); insight first painful then feeling better (Lipkin, 1954; 2/8)
	Feeling Empowered	Self-confident, strength within (Rodgers, 2002; Klein & Elliott, 2006; Lipkin, 1954); general sense of well-being: health, energy, activities (Klein & Elliott, 2006); newfound or improved abilities to act (Klein & Elliott, 2006); improved general day-to-day coping (Dale et al., 1998); giving self-credit for accomplishments, try new things, reading (Elliott, 2002); improved ability to cope (Elliott et al., 1990); preparing to take action to deal with problems (Elliott et al., 1990); specific wishes/attitudes strengthened (Elliott et al., 1990); being able to make decisions, gaining control over life (Timulak et al., 2009; Lipkin, 1954; Rodgers, 2002); able to stand up for self, more initiative instead of fear of doing things (Lipkin, 1954; 7/8)

(continues)

TABLE 4.4. Example of Hierarchically Structured Metacategories of Client-Reported Outcomes in Person-Centered/Experiential Therapies (*Continued*)

Main metacategory	Metacategories	Primary studies' findings
	Mastering Symptoms	Can cross bridges, can fly (Elliott et al., 2009); symptoms went one by one, sudden relief (Lipkin, 1954; 2/8)
	Enjoying Change in Circumstances	Improved nonrelationship aspects of life independent of therapy (Elliott et al., 1990; Elliott, 2002a; 2/8)
Appreciating Experience of Self in Relationship With Others	Feeling Supported	Feeling respected by children, seeking support group (Klein & Elliott, 2006). Note: Reported changes in others' view of self (Elliott et al., 1990); people tell me I am a nicer person (Elliott et al., 2009). In many studies, attributions to therapy/ therapist as providers of support (3/8)
	Enjoying Interpersonal Encounters	Better interpersonal functioning (all, romantic, family; Klein & Elliott, 2006); reordering relationships (Dale et al., 1998); being able to cope with reactions of others (Timulak at al., 2009); increased independence/assertion (Elliott et al., 1990); increased positive openness (Elliott et al., 1990); improved relationships (Elliott et al., 1990); better relationship with my wife, more tolerant (Elliott et al., 2009; 5/8)
Changed View of Self/Others	Self-Insight and Self-Awareness	Development of meaning and understanding of abuse, learning from therapy (Dale et al., 1998; Lipkin, 1954); more aware of and true to myself (Klein & Elliott, 2006); realizations about self (Elliott et al., 1990); enlightened (problem fitting in like a glove), better understanding self (I am not in the dark, I can do something about it); seeing patterns (Lipkin, 1954; 4/8)
	Changed View of Others	See other viewpoints (Klein & Elliott, 2006); being more interested in others (Timulak et al., 2009); changes in client's views and attitudes toward others (Elliott et al., 1990); accepting parent faults (Timulak et al., 2009; 3/8)

Note. The citations in this table are in the original table, and readers who are interested in any of the cited articles may consult Timulak and Creaner (2010). From "Qualitative Meta-Analysis of Outcomes of Person-Centred/Experiential Therapies," by L. Timulak and M. Creaner, in M. Cooper, J. C. Watson, and D. Hölldampf (Eds.), *Person-Centred and Experiential Psychotherapies Work* (pp. 76–77), 2010, PCCS Books. Copyright 2010 by L. Timulak and M. Creaner. Reprinted with permission.

to working with meta-analyses of approximately 20 studies (but see Levitt et al., 2016, who meta-analyzed 109 studies), where the number and the format of MUs may differ to the extent that this type of presentation is not necessarily feasible. Hence, these examples are intended to offer an idea to the reader of possible table presentations of a QMA, but they are not the only way a QMA can display metacategories. The display of metacategories operating with larger numbers of primary studies may simply represent the numbers of studies that contributed to the metacategory (the actual cross-reference of those studies may be provided in an electronic supplement to the QMA; see Ladmanová et al., 2021).

Another important point is that although we refer to the final outline of a QMA's result as being in the format of metacategories (potentially hierar-chically organized), it is not a requirement that QMA results are displayed this way. We are supporters of a *generic approach* to qualitative research (Elliott & Timulak, 2021), which means that the procedures we outline here are only illustrative and are not intended to be prescriptive. We encourage meta-analysts to consider what format their ultimate presentation of find-ings should take. The aesthetic as well as pragmatic considerations may be important, together with how the primary studies presented their find-ings and the discipline-specific traditions within which the QMA is situated. Thus, the term *metacategory* or its format (a very short description of the meaning captured by clustered MUs) is not necessarily a requirement. The meta-analyst can discuss, for instance, metathemes, or they may need to present their results in the form of (abbreviated) descriptions.

For instance, in their QMA, which examined processes in significant events leading to insight on the part of the client, Timulak and McElvaney (2013) presented findings in the form of descriptions (narratives) that were signifi-cantly shortened for the table presentation. Table 4.5 presents their findings in the form of short descriptions across the nine domains (represented by nine cells in the table). These domains (also presented in Table 4.2) structure the phenomenon of therapeutic events that led to insight across the actors/ reflectors of the process (Client's Process, Therapist Process, and Client–Therapist Interaction) and chronologically (Context, Event and Key Inter-vention, and Impact), creating a 3 × 3 window. The actual findings are brief descriptions within the domains/cells in the table. They were supplemented by a thorough narrative description in the main body of the Results section of the article and contained quotes from the therapy sessions or the postsession client and therapist recollections (see Timulak & McElvaney, 2013).

It is interesting that in Timulak and McElvaney's (2013) QMA we also discovered that there were essentially two types of significant events that led to two distinct types of impacts (insights). The first insight was that clients

TABLE 4.5. Example Qualitative Meta-Analysis Findings in the Form of Short Descriptions/Narratives: Processes Involved in Painful/Poignant Insight Events

	Client process (intent, expressed content, emotional experience, reflection)	Therapist process (intent, intervention, reflection/observation)	Therapist and client interaction
Context (Lead-In to the Event)	• Client vulnerable (Elliott, 1983, 1984; Elliott & Shapiro, 1992; Elliott et al., 1994; Hardy et al., 1998; Labott et al., 1992; 6/6) • A core issue worked on in therapy (Elliott, 1983, 1984; Elliott & Shapiro, 1992; Elliott et al., 1994; Hardy et al., 1998; Labott et al., 1992; 6/6) • Client requesting help to self-understand (Elliott, 1984; Elliott et al., 1994; Hardy et al., 1998; Labott et al., 1992; 4/6)	• Therapist focuses on theoretically informed therapeutic strategy (Elliott, 1983, 1984; Elliott & Shapiro, 1992; Elliott et al., 1994; Hardy et al., 1998; Labott et al., 1992; 6/6) • Therapist sees client as ready for intervention (interpretation; Elliott, 1984; 1/6) • Therapist confident, empathic, and in charge (Hardy et al., 1998; 1/6) • Therapist self-critical about the progress of therapy (Elliott, 1983; 1/6)	• Therapeutic alliance is good (Elliott et al., 1994; Hardy et al., 1998; Labott et al., 1992; 3/6) • Therapist sees client as avoiding (Elliott & Shapiro, 1992; Hardy et al., 1998; 2/6)
Event and Key Intervention	• Client feeling vulnerable/distressed (Elliott, 1983, 1984; Elliott & Shapiro, 1992; Elliott et al., 1994; Hardy et al., 1998; Labott et al., 1992; 6/6) • Client shares own insight (Elliott, 1983; Labott et al., 1992; 2/6) • Client finds therapist helpful (Elliott, 1983, 1984; Hardy et al., 1998; 3/6)	• Therapist shows empathic understanding (Elliott, 1983; Elliott & Shapiro, 1992; Hardy et al., 1998; 3/6) • Therapist interprets (Elliott, 1983, 1984; Elliott et al., 1994; 3/6) • Therapist softens the intervention (Elliott, 1983, 1984; Elliott et al., 1994; 3/6) • Therapist imperfect (Elliott, 1983, 1984; 2/6) • Therapist provides process guidance (Hardy et al., 1998; 1/6)	• Disruptions in alliance (Elliott et al., 1994; Hardy et al., 1994; Elliott & Shapiro, 1992; Labott et al., 1992; 4/6) • Empathic flow/collaborative element (Elliott, 1983, 1984; Elliott et al., 1994; Hardy et al., 1998; 4/6) • Therapist softens the intervention, and client tolerates it (Elliott, 1983; Elliott, 1984; Elliott et al., 1994; 3/6) • Key response contained important words used by client (Elliott, 1983; Elliott & Shapiro, 1992; Elliott et al., 1994; Hardy et al., 1998; Labott et al., 1992; 5/6)

| Impact/ Consequences | • Painful/poignant/moving awareness/insight (Elliott, 1983, 1984; Elliott & Shapiro, 1992; Elliott et al., 1994; Hardy et al., 1998; Labott et al., 1992; 6/6)

 • Client works further with the impact (awareness/insight; Elliott, 1983, 1984; Elliott & Shapiro, 1992; Elliott et al., 1994; Labott et al., 1992; Hardy et al., 1998; 6/6)

 • Client feels connection with therapist (Elliott, 1983, 1984; Elliott & Shapiro, 1992; Hardy et al., 1998; Labott et al., 1992; 5/6)

 • Relief (Elliott, 1984; Elliott & Shapiro, 1992; 2/6)

 • Avoidance (Elliott & Shapiro, 1992; Labott et al., 1992; 2/6)

 • Disagreement with therapist (Elliott, 1983; Elliott & Shapiro, 1992; 2/6)

 • Client hopeful about therapy (Elliott, 1983; Hardy et al., 1998; Labott et al., 1992; 3/6) | • Therapist puts emphasis on cognitive insight (Elliott, 1983; Elliott & Shapiro, 1992; Hardy et al., 1998; Labott et al., 1992; 4/6)

 • Therapist sees client as avoiding (Elliott & Shapiro, 1992; Hardy et al., 1998; Labott et al., 1992; 3/6)

 • Some impacts go unnoticed by therapist (Elliott, 1984; Labott et al., 1992; 2/6) | • Therapist puts emphasis on cognitive insight and client stresses emotionally painful insight (Elliott, 1983; Elliott & Shapiro, 1992; Hardy et al., 1998; Labott et al., 1992; 4/6)

 • Alliance enhanced (Elliott, 1983, 1984; Hardy et al., 1998; 3/6)

 • Client agrees with therapist (Elliott, 1984; Elliott et al., 1994; 2/6)

 • Therapist deflects further work (Elliott, 1984; Elliott et al., 1994; 2/6)

 • Strains in alliance (Elliott et al., 1994; 1/6) |

Note. The citations in this table are in the original table, and readers who are interested in any of the cited articles may consult Timulak and McElvaney (2013). From "Qualitative Meta-Analysis of Insight Events in Psychotherapy," by L. Timulak and R. McElvaney, 2013, *Counselling Psychology Quarterly*, 26(2), pp. 11–12 (https://doi.org/10.1080/09515070.2013.792997). Copyright 2013 by Taylor & Francis Ltd. Adapted with permission.

experienced it as painful, but they also considered it helpful (e.g., deepened self-understanding), and the second type of insight was more empowering, promoting assertiveness. The processes in the two types of events also differed. Hence, Timulak and McElvaney ended the QMA by presenting the two types of events that led to insight; the second one is presented in Table 4.6. Thus, the nature of the phenomenon, how it was studied in the primary studies, and, ultimately, the QMA findings were conducive to presenting the results in two different types of events, each based on a number of studies and a number of events (overall, the QMA was based on seven studies that among themselves included 15 significant insight events). The display of findings in this particular QMA illustrates the flexibility in format that findings may take in a QMA. The final format of the findings may depend on many factors, such as pragmatic and aesthetic considerations, as well as the phenomenon itself, as well as the format of results in the primary studies. Again, in both of these examples we also see references to the original primary studies.

REPRESENTATIVENESS OF METACATEGORIES

Tables 4.3 through 4.6 show how representative each metacategory was with reference to the sample of primary studies. These specific tables also list the exact original studies that contributed to each metacategory (not how many participants or events because the number of participants or events in the original primary studies may differ). We recommend this step in a QMA. It corresponds to the enumeration of categories with reference to its representativeness within a sample (participants) of an individual qualitative study (Timulak & Elliott, 2019). It tells the reader how frequently the finding is captured by a metacategory among the selected studies (see an example in Table 4.7). Given that we also know the characteristics of the primary studies (e.g., size and characteristics of the samples in the original studies), enumeration of the studies to which our metacategories pertain gives the reader contextual information that may be relevant to the discussion of and reflection on the findings.

Other QMA methodologists also recommend sharing with the reader the representativeness of each metacategory of the primary studies (Sandelowski & Barroso, 2003). Sandelowski and Barroso (2003) also suggested looking at the final findings from the perspective of the individual studies. They advised providing information on how many QMA metacategories were contributed to by an individual primary study. This tells the reader about the richness and influence of a particular primary study. Thus, we can assess,

TABLE 4.6. Example of Qualitative Meta-Analysis Findings in the Form of Short Descriptions/Narratives: Processes Involved in Self-Assertive/Empowering Insight Events

	Client process (intent, expressed content, emotional experience, reflection)	Therapist process (intent, intervention, reflection/observation)	Therapist and client interaction
Context (lead-in to the event)	• A core issue worked on in therapy (Elliott et al., 1994; Rees et al., 2001); two out of two studies (2/2) • Client vulnerable (Elliott et al., 1994; Rees et al., 2001; 2/2)	• Therapist focuses on theoretically informed therapeutic strategy stressing assertion of needs (Elliott et al., 1994; Rees et al., 2001; 2/2)	• Collaborative therapeutic alliance although with some limits (Elliott et al., 1994; Rees et al., 2001; 2/2)
Event and key intervention	• Client follows therapist suggestion (Elliott et al., 1994; Rees et al., 2001; 2/2)	• Therapist supportive, validating, collaborative, providing reframing promoting positive experience (Elliott et al., 1994; Rees et al., 2001; 2/2) • Provides guidance in specific steps (Rees et al., 2001)	• Collaborative work following CBT theoretical agenda (Elliott et al., 1994; Rees et al., 2001; 2/2)
Impact/consequences	• Awareness of personal needs/wants (Elliott et al., 1994; Rees et al., 2001; 2/2) Painful awareness (Rees et al., 2001; 1/2) • Insight emerges serendipitously (Elliott et al., 1994; 1/2) • Feeling understood (Elliott et al., 1994; 1/2) • Feeling relieved (Elliott et al., 1994; 1/2)	• Therapist plans further work on self-assertion and reframing (Rees et al., 2001; 1/2)	• Client agrees with therapist's appraisal and strategy, and both work on its implementation (Elliott et al., 1994; Rees et al., 2001; 2/2) • Client agrees with therapist's appraisal and strategy, and both work on its implementation (Elliott et al., 1994; Rees et al., 2001; 2/2)

Note. The citations in this table are in the original table, and readers who are interested in any of the cited articles may consult Timulak and McElvaney (2013). CBT = cognitive behavior therapy. From "Qualitative Meta-Analysis of Insight Events in Psychotherapy," by L. Timulak and R. McElvaney, 2013, *Counselling Psychology Quarterly*, 26(2), p. 13 (https://doi.org/10.1080/09515070.2013.792997). Copyright 2013 by Taylor & Francis Ltd. Adapted with permission.

TABLE 4.7. Example of Qualitative Meta-Analysis Findings of the Most and Least Representative Metacategories of Helpful Aspects of Eating Disorder Treatment

Metacategory	Primary studies' findings
Feeling Understood/ Being Listened to/ Having Opportunity to Talk[a]	Feeling understood (Banasiak et al., 2007; Button & Warren, 2001; Cockell et al., 2004; Colton & Pistrang, 2004; Dunn et al., 2006; Moreno et al., 1995; Rorty et al., 1993; Roy et al., 2006), being heard (Colton & Pistrang, 2004), being empathically listened to (Banasiak et al., 2007; Colton & Pistrang, 2004; Dunn et al., 2006; Le Grange & Gelman, 1998; Ma, 2008; Offord et al., 2006; Reid et al., 2008; Rorty et al., 1993; Roy et al., 2006), having opportunity to talk [openly] to the mental health professional (Banasiak et al., 2007; Button & Warren, 2001; Cockell et al., 2004; Le Grange & Gelman, 1998; Reid et al., 2008; Roy et al., 2006), could reduce isolation and loneliness (Banasiak et al., 2007; Colton & Pistrang, 2004; 12/24)
Importance of Follow-Up Interventions[b]	Follow-up interventions and possibility of staying in touch with mental health professionals (Cockell et al., 2004; Offord et al., 2006; 2/24)

Note. The citations in this table are in the original table, and readers who are interested in any of the cited articles may consult Timulak et al. (2013). From *Helpful and Unhelpful Aspects of Eating Disorders Treatment Involving Psychological Therapy: A Meta-Synthesis of Qualitative Research Studies* (pp. 35–36), by L. Timulak, J. Buckroyd, J. Klimas, M. Creaner, D. Wellsted, F. Bunn, S. Bradshaw, and G. Green, 2013, British Association for Counselling and Psychotherapy (https://www.bacp.co.uk/media/1980/bacp-helpful-unhelpful-aspects-eating-disorders-treatment-involving-psychological-therapies.pdf). Copyright 2013 by British Association for Counselling and Psychotherapy. Adapted with permission.
[a]Twelve out of 24 primary studies contributed to this metacategory. [b]Two out of 24 primary studies contributed to this metacategory.

for instance, whether the whole QMA is based primarily on a handful of studies. For instance, in Timulak et al.'s (2013) QMA there were, overall, 29 (primary-order) metacategories of helpful aspects of ED treatment. There were also 18 metacategories that captured the unhelpful aspects of ED treatment (the QMA was based on 24 studies that involved cumulative data from 1,058 participants). If we picked a particular primary study—say, Banasiak et al. (2007)—we can see that it contributed to 15 helpful and 10 unhelpful aspects of ED treatment metacategories. Therefore, Banasiak et al.'s study had a significant influence on the final outline of the QMA. In comparison, Rorty et al.'s (1993) study had a more modest impact: It contributed to seven helpful and three unhelpful aspects of ED treatment metacategories. This can be perhaps explained by the fact that Banasiak et al.'s study focused on clients' satisfaction with treatment, whereas Rorty et al.'s study focused on the broader recovery process (and not necessarily on experiences of treatment).

Thus, Banasiak et al.'s study focus was more closely aligned with the focus of the QMA and provided more relevant data than Rorty et al.'s study.

ASSESSING THE IMPACT OF METHODOLOGICAL FEATURES OF THE PRIMARY STUDIES ON THE QUANTITATIVE META-ANALYSIS

In Chapter 3, we stressed that the critical appraisal of selected studies not only serves selection purposes but is actually a part of data analysis. First of all, it is important to know how the phenomenon is examined by a QMA study, and, second, we want to see what impact the methodological features (e.g., the method of data collection, the method of data analysis, the participants, the theoretical background of the primary researchers) of the primary studies have on the QMA findings. Thus, we recommend that the Results section of a QMA first report on how the phenomenon is studied but also assess what impact methodology may have had on the outcomes. For instance, in their QMA of helpful and unhelpful aspects of ED treatment, Timulak et al. (2013) observed that the majority of studies (17 out of 24) used semistructured interviews, and five used written responses to the questions in questionnaires (the remaining studies used other formats of data collection, e.g., focus groups). We observed that the studies that used written accounts provided fewer findings ("thinner" data), which made assessing them and comparing them with the rest of the data more difficult. Our reading of these data thus had to be more inferential, and we had less confidence in our understanding of the original studies' categorization/findings. The assessment of the impact that methodological features have on the findings of QMA was recommended by Paterson et al. (2001) in their metastudy description of QMA. We see the potential for this type of assessment to be made more explicit and used in future QMAs in psychology.

CREDIBILITY CHECKS

Similar to individual qualitative studies, a QMA can benefit from *credibility checks*, that is, strategies or procedures to enhance the methodological integrity and quality of the research. We believe credibility checks can enrich QMAs and contribute to the confidence the reader has in the QMA. The meta-analysts themselves, as well as the reader, can thus build trust in the overall quality of a particular QMA (see the concept of trustworthiness of qualitative studies in Morrow, 2005).

Credibility checks can be used at every stage of a QMA. Some may be used by individual members of the meta-analysts' team because the QMA is often a team effort, and some may rely on the perspective of the colleagues from outside the meta-analysts' team (for a discussion of team work in qualitative research, see Vivino et al., 2012). We also recommend the use of an *auditor*, a person who oversees individual steps of the QMA and critically appraises them. In the context of a doctoral dissertation, the research supervisor often assumes the role of auditor. The auditor can inspect every single step of the QMA study—from the selection process, data localization/extraction, delineation of the MUs, through to the creation of the metacategories. In such a case, the auditor should then have access to all the data. Usually, at every step the auditor provides feedback and discusses any suggested changes.

For instance, when we are deciding on the initial research problem and research questions, we can use team discussion or seek opinions from outside the prospective meta-analysts' group on the initial formulation of the research problem and research questions. Feedback on the initial research problem formulation and research questions may also be sought informally, from a colleague, or formally, from a fellow meta-analyst who would assume the role of auditor. Similarly, once we start the study selection, the process of deciding on the key words for selecting primary studies can benefit from consultations within the team or outside the team. The actual selection of primary studies, running the literature searches, and hand-searching abstracts and full texts can benefit from credibility checks. For instance, if we operate within a team of meta-analysts, two team members can run the searches independently, or, when initial studies/hits are localized, further scrutiny may be divided between the team members in a way that at least a portion of identified studies can be overlapped and seen by at least two meta-analysts. Thus, we can establish whether there is a chance of missing studies or whether the meta-analysts who are scrutinizing studies essentially select the same studies from the shared pool of studies they reviewed. Delineation of the MUs can also benefit from a credibility check and may be at least examined in part by an auditor or an assigned rater (another team member). The same applies to clustering of the MUs into metacategories and then to the development of metacategory names. The metacategory names can be tried out on potential readers (colleagues) to see whether they understand the meaning they are trying to capture.

Another procedure to potentially enhance credibility is seeking feedback and validation of the QMA findings from the researchers/authors of the primary studies. This is akin to member checking in individual qualitative studies, whereby the researcher contacts the participants to validate the findings of the study. However, contacting the researchers of the primary studies (in this case or, more generally, to clarify information related to a primary study, etc.) may not be that practical an approach for a variety of reasons (e.g., the primary researchers may be unavailable, the process of dialoguing with them may be time consuming, the primary researchers may not be interested in discussing the QMA).

Various forms of *triangulation* (a combination of methods, data sources, analysts, or perspectives in qualitative research; Patton, 1999) also can be done, not only by using various perspectives (e.g., researchers, auditors, the use of a QMA team; Hill et al., 2012) or assessment of the study characteristics and their impact on the QMA findings but also, if suitable, by using independent raters outside the original team. For instance, the metacategories that represent findings of a QMA can be transformed into a taxonomy (of metacategories and their definitions). This taxonomy that can serve as a nominal scale, and independent raters (to whom the goals of the QMA should be kept unknown) can be asked to use the taxonomy (now a nominal scale) and sort out the MUs (the same MUs that were initially examined and were used to build the taxonomy from the bottom up) to the existing metacategories. Involving independent raters can thus provide an increased quality assurance and confidence in the process.

Credibility checks, together with other procedures (e.g., the situatedness of the meta-analysts, the quality of presentation, resonance of the findings), all contribute to the overall methodological integrity of the QMA (Levitt, Motulsky, et al., 2017; we comment further on this in Chapters 5 and 6). It is therefore important that these checks are well documented. The meta-analysts can keep a reflective diary or journal in which they document how their QMA process unfolded and what checks they used at every stage of their QMA. We highly recommend that this documenting is done contemporaneously for each step and each decision taken therein—otherwise, the detail and rationale may get lost as the QMA progresses. Any new angle, any new information that a check brings, can potentially enrich the meta-analysts' perspective on the studied phenomenon and can increase the meta-analysts' ownership of their study and their confidence in its presentation.

SUMMARY

The data in the QMA are organized through a conceptual framework (domains of investigation), and data preparation is analyzed through data categorization. Again, a flexible and iterative approach is emphasized throughout the

QMA process; one step may refine, shape, or influence the next step or a preceding step. The examples of the presentation of findings we have discussed in this chapter show that there is variability in how the findings are ultimately captured and presented. Therefore, future meta-analysts do not need to be limited in how they approach their analysis process and the final look of their findings. We also highlighted how the researchers (of the primary studies and of the QMA) may potentially influence the outcomes of their studies, and we stress the importance of making explicit the interpretative framework of both the primary studies and the QMA. Finally, we emphasize that credibility checks are important for methodological integrity as well as for the reader's confidence in the QMA procedures.

5 LIMITATIONS AND CHALLENGES OF QUALITATIVE META-ANALYSIS

So far, we have primarily focused on how to conduct a qualitative meta-analysis (QMA). In this chapter, we focus on some of the limitations and challenges meta-analysts may encounter at various stages of a QMA. We also discuss the meta-analysts' ethical responsibilities, and, finally, we make a case for striving for high methodological integrity throughout the whole process of conducting a QMA.

QUALITY OF THE PRIMARY STUDIES

One of the first limitations of any QMA is the quality of studies that are included in it (Thorne et al., 2004). In an individual qualitative study, one can always improve the data collection method, the interview schedule, interviewing style, or the quality of observations. In a QMA, however, the meta-analysts are always dependent on the quality of the overall work of the researchers who conducted the primary studies and on the quality of their presented findings.

The field of qualitative research is evolving, and standards are being formulated (e.g., Elliott et al., 1999; Levitt et al., 2018; Levitt, Motulsky, et al., 2017), so there should be an expectation that published qualitative studies

https://doi.org/10.1037/0000313-005
Essentials of Qualitative Meta-Analysis, by L. Timulak and M. Creaner

encompass appropriate methodological standards and report on them clearly and sufficiently. However, a QMA is based on the fact that it typically covers *all* the relevant primary studies meta-analysts were able to locate. Therefore, a QMA may also include studies published in lower impact journals or non-mainstream journals or journals from disciplines whose expectations regarding methodology and writing up results may differ from those of psychology journals, so the quality or style of the primary studies will inevitably vary. However, rigorously appraising the methodological features of the primary studies and having a threshold for methodological requirements for the inclusion of a study can, to some extent, help address the issue of problematic quality (or insufficient information on the methodology used; see our discussion of this issue in Chapter 3, in the Appraisal of Primary Studies section). Nevertheless, the meta-analysts likely will be confronted with this type of limitation and must address such limitations to the extent that it is possible.

In our experience (Timulak & Creaner, 2013), we occasionally have found studies included in our QMAs in which the analysis or findings were not fully clear. We do not want to single out any such examples specifically, so we will illustrate the problems with a hypothetical example. Let us say that we are conducting a QMA to examine client posttherapy reported experiences of helpful and unhelpful aspects of therapy, and we locate a primary study in which the researchers asked a small number of clients to complete posttherapy questionnaires. The primary study's description of the analysis says only that a content analysis was conducted, but it does not indicate by whom and does not say anything about the researchers' or analysts' background. The brief Results section presents themes that are each captured by one word (a noun), making it difficult to understand the theme. The study authors report how many times a theme was mentioned but do not indicate how many participants mentioned the theme. Some themes are supplemented by quotes; some are not. The ones without illustrative quotes may simply read "Talking." Thus, we know that clients found "talking" to be helpful in therapy, but we do not know what was helpful about the talking (e.g., was talking helpful because otherwise the clients would have kept the problems to themselves, and that is burdensome for them; was talking helpful because otherwise nobody listens; was talking helpful because the client could share with the therapist a troubling experience; was talking helpful because therapy was exploratory [rather than prescriptive], so the client could talk about whatever they wanted rather than having to do prescribed activities/exercises?).

In addition to descriptions often being too short and ambiguous, we also have encountered a problem whereby the primary studies used illustrative quotes, but these quotes do not seem to fit the theme they are supposedly illustrating (or at least they do not illustrate the theme in a straightforward manner we can understand). For instance, there is a theme labeled "Relationship" (as a helpful aspect of therapy) but a quote saying something like "It was good that I could finally talk about my problems." This quote does not illustrate the "Relationship" theme in a clear and unambiguous manner. Similarly, we can have the same theme, but it captures experiences with the very opposite connotation (e.g., a theme named "Relationship" listed under both helpful aspects and unhelpful aspects of therapy in the same primary study—meaning that the same theme actually refers to opposite experiences, i.e., the helpful and the unhelpful role of the therapeutic relationship in therapy).

Another problem we have come across is that the primary researchers used a brand name method (e.g., grounded theory) but did not provide detail about the procedures used to conduct the analysis. Referencing a brand name method does not say much about the actual procedures of the particular study. Researchers claiming to follow the same brand name method may actually follow different procedures, whereas researchers claiming the use of different brand name approaches may actually be similar (a metastudy conducted by Levitt, Pomerville, et al., 2017, illustrates this; for a longer discussion of this issue, see Elliott & Timulak, 2021, and Timulak & Elliott, 2019).

Although the quality of primary studies poses a serious challenge to a QMA, we are hopeful that the standard of qualitative studies is improving with qualitative methodology becoming a more central part of psychology training and guidelines for the reporting of qualitative studies now available (Levitt et al., 2017; Levitt, Motulsky, et al., 2017). Our experience has been that a minority of studies have had these types of problems, and we have been able to resolve these issues by engaging them thorough considerations about the impact of these types of problems on the QMA. It was also our experience that the "problematic" primary studies were usually "thinner" (less informative) in regard to the relevant data and thus did not affect any QMAs we have conducted in any major way.

OTHER LIMITATIONS OF QUALITATIVE META-ANALYSES

The typical limitation of a QMA noted by many QMA methodologists (e.g., Paterson et al., 2001; Sandelowski & Barroso, 2006; Walsh & Downe, 2005) refers to the meta-analysts' remoteness from the actual data in the primary studies. The fear is that the contextual and nuanced understanding that qualitative methods offer is not fully used, and thus something from an important context may be lost. This can definitely be the case, but one has to also be aware that the purpose of a QMA is different from the purpose of an individual qualitative study. In a primary study, the researchers investigate the phenomenon at hand in an attempt to achieve an in-depth, nuanced understanding of that phenomenon. In a QMA, the meta-analysts want to obtain a comprehensive, summative picture of the findings of a pool of primary studies that have investigated the same phenomenon (although it is the phenomenon on which the primary studies focused and whose nuances they investigated). Therefore, although the primary studies focus on depth and nuances, a QMA focuses on the comprehensiveness and definite features of the overall picture. The problem of missing nuances in the QMA is shared with quantitative meta-analysis and so is characteristic of the meta-analysis method (and systematic reviews) more broadly. We want to mitigate this issue to an extent also by examining how some study characteristics affect the results of the meta-analysis (e.g., in-depth interviews used in the primary studies may yield data richer than those of studies that used written questionnaires). Yet the QMA may be potentially missing some more contextual and nuanced findings.

Another potential problem relates to including primary studies that used different methodological approaches (Atkins et al., 2008). We are aware that there may be limits to what sort of qualitative methods used in the primary studies can be meta-analyzed together. In Chapter 3, in our discussion of inclusion and exclusion criteria, we pointed out that this consideration has to be made and that limits can be set on the methodological features of the studies that would meet the inclusion criteria. So, for instance, for the purposes of a particular study, we can accept broadly defined descriptive and interpretive qualitative approaches but exclude language- and conversation-based approaches (e.g., discourse analysis or conversation analysis). On the other hand, at times it may be possible to include even quite disparate methods. For example, Timulak et al. (2013) focused on 24 primary studies, which were all variants of a typical descriptive-interpretive approach to qualitative research (e.g., grounded theory, interpretative phenomenological analysis, thematic analysis) and one discourse–analytical study that was quite distinct in its focus on discursive rules and practices. Nonetheless, they were able to distill some relevant data from the latter that fit the focus of the QMA. Therefore, they included that study, although its contribution to the body of data was minimal.

Future QMAs most likely will need to grapple with the issue of combining or not combining primary studies using methods that are based on divergent epistemological positions. In any case, conducting a QMA requires that at least some members of the meta-analysts' research team have solid knowledge of qualitative methodology and genres of qualitative research because it is to be expected that there will be considerations around setting a boundary in regard to what sort of methodology will meet the QMA's inclusion criteria (see the section titled The Person of the Meta-Analyst in Chapter 2).

Another issue we want to highlight (which is not really a specific limitation of QMA) is that QMAs are covering only what is being studied and not what is *not* being studied. Consequently, underrepresented voices that may not be the focus of many studies may remain so in the summative accounts provided by QMAs. One way of addressing this is obviously to expand the breadth of the primary studies. This is not fully in the hands of meta-analysts. What can be in the hands of meta-analysts, though, is ensuring representation and diversity on the research team.

ETHICAL CONSIDERATIONS

The meta-analysts normally work with published studies and, hence, secondary data. They typically have no direct responsibility to ensure that the treatment of participants in primary studies followed expected ethical standards, yet examining information on the ethical considerations reported in the primary studies is something that should be a part of their critical appraisal of the studies. Malterud (2019) advocated for a thorough review of the available information on the ethical approval given to and the ethical procedures followed in the primary studies. Malterud suggested that if such information on ethics is missing in the published record, the meta-analysts consider whether any quotes from these primary studies should be used as illustrative quotes in the QMA.

Further ethical considerations are warranted if the meta-analysts used the primary studies' original data sets. We do not discuss this option in this book, beyond our remark in Chapter 3 (p. 33; also see McCormick et al., 2003), because this is not something commonly done in a QMA. However, even though the combination of the primary studies' data sets is a rare occurrence in a QMA, it nonetheless is a possibility (for use in a quantitative meta-analysis; e.g., Eisenhauer, 2021). If the meta-analysts were in fact meta-analyzing varied original data sets from the primary studies, the original ethics information (approval, information sheets, consent forms) in the primary studies would have to explicitly allow for such an option. With the growing emphasis on open science, this may be possible; however, ethical considerations (e.g., the virtual impossibility of anonymizing data) and responsibilities of the meta-analysts would then be very complex (see Irwin, 2013).

An additional and important point regarding ethical considerations relates to the ethical integrity of the meta-analysts' overall approach. Given that some QMAs may have an impact on practice and policy developments, it is very important that any potential conflicts of interest on the part of the meta-analysts are considered and transparently handled. For instance, if the meta-analysts examine clients' experience of a particular form of psychotherapy, it is important to explicitly state whether any of the meta-analysts is a developer of that particular therapy. The transparency of preregistering a QMA, and the use of credibility checks (auditors, research team, independent raters), as well as the review process in scientific journals, should contribute to a sound and trustworthy QMA (see Chapter 2).

STRIVING FOR METHODOLOGICAL INTEGRITY

The recent recommendations of the American Psychological Association's Division 5, Qualitative and Quantitative Methods, promote the concept of *methodological integrity* for which each qualitative study should strive (Levitt, Motulsky, et al., 2017). Division 5 noted two pillars of methodological integrity: (a) fidelity to the subject matter (the phenomenon under investigation) and (b) utility in achieving the goals of the study. The whole book we present here is dedicated to outlining the procedures and tips that prospective meta-analysts should consider and the contemplation of which we hope contributes to the methodological integrity of a QMA. For instance, in terms of fidelity to the subject matter, meta-analysts should try to ensure they have all available data (the selection of studies and localization of relevant data within them) and that they analyze the data with a transparent and explicit framework that situates both the meta-analysts and the analytic procedures they follow. The product of the analysis should be adequately and sufficiently anchored in rich, illustrative examples. In terms of utility in achieving goals, we stress the importance of the appraisal of the primary studies' methodologies and how their methodologies could have affected their findings. We stress flexibility but also thoroughness in approaching the meta-analysis of the data (findings), so it fits the phenomenon under the investigation. We also stress the importance of having the final outline of the QMA findings displayed in a format that is coherent and clear to the reader. We are also aware of potential policy impacts of QMAs, given that they aspire to offer a summative and comprehensive perspective on a field or area of study, and therefore we stress the importance of rigor (e.g., credibility checks), transparency, and reflectivity in the QMA process.

SUMMARY

Despite the benefits of the QMA method and its potential utility and impact, there are limitations and challenges that must be considered. Most notably, the quality of a QMA ultimately relies on the quality of the primary studies included. Furthermore, there are ethical considerations in conducting a QMA, including the stance of striving for methodological integrity in each and every step throughout the entire QMA process.

6 PUBLISHING QUALITATIVE META-ANALYSES

In this chapter, we offer our perspectives on publishing a qualitative meta-analysis (QMA) that meta-analysts may find useful when preparing their QMA manuscript. We stress here the things that we believe were central to our experience of publishing several QMAs and going through the peer review process as well as being reviewers of other QMAs. There will obviously be some overlap with the recently published guidelines for the preparation of qualitative study manuscripts for American Psychological Association (APA) journals (see Levitt et al., 2018, 2019). These guidelines conveniently dedicate space specifically to QMAs (e.g., Qualitative Meta-Analysis Article Reporting Standards [QMARS], Levitt et al., 2018). An APA website provides also brief summaries of these reporting guidelines (https://apastyle.apa.org/jars/qual-table-2.pdf). Given that QMA is a form of systematic review, we urge you also to consult the Preferred Reporting Items for Systematic Reviews and Meta-Analyses (PRISMA) guidelines on reporting of systematic reviews (Page et al., 2021; https://www.prisma-statement.org). We encourage you to access these resources in conjunction with the tips we offer in this chapter. In the sections that follow, we offer our suggestions across

https://doi.org/10.1037/0000313-006
Essentials of Qualitative Meta-Analysis, by L. Timulak and M. Creaner
Copyright © 2023 by the American Psychological Association. All rights reserved.

the standard headings—Introduction, Method, Results, and Discussion— and expand on some of the key points discussed in previous chapters.

First, though, we offer a few comments on possible publication outlets for QMA studies. Again, given that QMA is a form of systematic review, journals that specialize in systematic reviews are obvious potential targets for submission. It is great to see that some of the mainstream journals that normally and primarily publish quantitative systematic reviews and quantitative meta-analyses are now publishing QMAs. For instance, Levitt et al. (2016) published their QMA on the clients' experiences of psychotherapy in *Psychological Bulletin*, and Almeida et al. (2019) published their theoretically informed QMA in *Clinical Psychology Review*. Journals that are traditionally open to qualitative research studies are often also open to QMAs.

The review process is often a daunting experience, but it allows the meta-analysts to see how their work is read (and at times we have found it has been misread!), so they can engage in dialogue with potential readers even when the submission is not successful. Meta-analysts can still get useful reactions and feedback that can help them shape their next submission attempt in a way that they would want the work to be understood and received. QMA (and qualitative research) is still a new genre, so reviewers may not be that familiar with benchmarks against which to compare it. However, how the editors and reviewers read and respond to a QMA paper may let the meta-analysts know whether they are being understood in their written account of their work. Overall, we believe that a good and important scholarly work will find an appropriate outlet, even if the process may be arduous at times. We encourage meta-analysts, when thinking about a potential platform for publishing their work, to primarily focus on what they want to communicate and to whom.

INTRODUCTION

The Introduction section of a QMA paper can be tricky and challenging to write. In the Introduction of a non–QMA empirical paper, we normally provide the rationale for our study on the basis of thorough knowledge (based on a thorough literature search) of a field of study. We summarize everything relevant that is known, evaluate that knowledge, identify the gaps, and thus establish a need for our study. In the case of a QMA, however, we want to reserve the thorough search for the next step in the project—that is, the selection of the relevant studies and the location of the relevant findings/ data in them—which is the equivalent of the data collection stage of an individual qualitative study. We need to capture the reader's attention at the outset and persuade them why there is a need for our QMA while not yet fully answering what is known in the field. We basically have to say something along the lines that there are indications in the field of study of an accumulation of studies that have examined the same problem or similar problems and that there is a need (practical, theoretical) to either summarize this accumulating qualitative research work or to resolve any contradictions in it (if there are suggestions that contradictions exist). At the same time, we need to respect the typical structure of an Introduction to the research paper, which includes providing context for the study, explaining the relevance of the QMA study in particular, the articulation of the research problem (what we need to address and resolve and why a QMA is the best way to do this), and specific research questions.

For example, in Timulak et al.'s (2013) QMA of helpful and unhelpful aspects of eating disorder treatment, we and our colleagues had to make a case as to why eating disorders are a problem and summarize how they are currently being treated. We also needed to establish what was already known from cumulative quantitative evidence about the treatment efficacy and effectiveness and what the treatment guidelines based on that evidence say. However, we also pointed to the fact that the service users' perspective is important to consider if one wants clients to be engaged in the treatment. This is something that the developers of treatment guidelines have also called for in the field, and there appears to be a body of qualitative studies that do provide information on the clients' perspective, in particular in terms of what they find helpful and unhelpful in their treatment. We thus articulated a rationale for a QMA that would systematically gather and analyze all the findings from qualitative studies that have examined the clients' perspectives of what they find helpful and unhelpful in their treatment. This research problem (how clients experience their treatment and what they find helpful and unhelpful) was then converted to the research question: What aspects of eating disorder treatment do clients find helpful or unhelpful?

Another relevant point in regard to some Introductions of QMA papers is that one of the legitimate reasons for conducting a QMA will be to update another, already-published QMA (France et al., 2016). Given that evidence (research findings) always evolves, and that systematic reviews (of which QMA is a variant) respond to this evolution, there is a natural need for updating QMAs. We have some experiences in this area as well (e.g., Ladmanová et al., 2021, which is partly an update and partly an expansion on a previous meta-analysis conducted by Timulak, 2007), and we expect that updates on already-existing QMAs will become more and more common with the growth of qualitative literature.

METHOD

The Method section typically references a particular QMA method that it followed (e.g., formal grounded theory, metastudy, metasummary), or it can reference a generic framework for the QMA as outlined in this book, for example. In any case, simply referencing a method (guide) that the QMA followed is insufficient. As we argued in Chapter 5, there is always a great potential for significant variability in how the meta-analysts apply the same "QMA method" or the same "QMA procedure" to which they refer. Thus, we urge meta-analysts, apart from citing some QMA description (like the one in this book), to describe their procedures in detail. Such detail may become common knowledge at some point, but QMA is still a relatively unknown method.

The Method section should also include the theoretical, professional, and personal background of the meta-analysts given that this background shapes their decisions about research questions; study selection criteria; definition of the data; and in particular their reading of, interpreting of, and reporting on (analyzing) the data. The meta-analysts can situate themselves by succinctly sharing their background or by explicitly anchoring their study in a particular theoretical framework that in itself provides that information (Hissa & Timulak, 2020) or by combination of both.

In addition, as we mentioned in Chapter 3, we recommend preregistering the QMA protocol in a systematic reviews registry, such as the International Prospective Register of Systematic Reviews (PROSPERO; https://www.crd.york.ac.uk/prospero/), and refer to it in the Method section, so the reader can see what the meta-analysts planned at the start of the study and how they updated their protocol, if they did so, during their QMA.

In terms of the literature search, we strongly recommend reporting on the exact search strategy (e.g., Boolean search) used in the QMA. In terms of reporting on the scrutiny of studies selected for the QMA, we recommend using the PRISMA flow chart (see Chapter 3 and the next section, Results, of this chapter). The meta-analysts should also consider the use (and report on it) of formal criteria for assessing the studies' eligibility (in terms of methodological requirements; again, see Chapter 3 for more detail). Clarity on which primary studies characteristics were collected and appraised should also be provided. A thorough description of the analytic process (e.g., following the steps outlined in this book), together with a clear description of the credibility checks undertaken, is imperative. It is important that there is some assessment of how the methodological characteristics of primary studies influence the QMA results. This is a natural part of the analysis process, and the procedure for how it was done should be reported on in the Method section.

RESULTS

According to PRISMA (Page et al., 2021) recommendations, the Results section starts with the flowchart of the selection process (a PRISMA diagram can be used; see https://www.prisma-statement.org), followed by a presentation of the characteristics of the primary studies. Although the APA's Qualitative Meta-Analysis Article Reporting Standards (QMARS; Levitt, 2018) recommend mentioning both of those in the Method section, the PRISMA guidelines recommend placing this in the Results section (see Cuijpers, 2016). Study characteristics often offer important insights into how the phenomenon that a QMA investigates was studied, which may be a finding in and of itself. For example, in a recent QMA on clinical supervision that investigated the helpful and unhelpful aspects of individual supervision, Chircop Coleiro et al. (2022) noted that few primary studies reported on the training and theoretical background of the supervisors. This observation may on its own contribute to recommendations for primary researchers to include such contextual information (about the background of the supervisors) in future research.

The main part of the Results section is naturally devoted to the actual findings of the QMA. We dedicated a lot of space to this in Chapter 4 in our discussion of the format of the findings (i.e., domains of investigation [what we wanted to study] vs. metacategories [what we found]). In Chapter 4, we addressed other important points relevant to the presentation of findings in the Results section. These include emphasizing the importance of the suitable names for the metacategories (e.g., their symmetry, succinctness, catchiness); a potential need for a hierarchical organization of metacategories; and consideration of other formats of presenting the findings, such as narratives.

We strongly recommend the use of tables to display findings because they allow readers to orient themselves to the findings expediently, and the visual aid of a table increases accessibility of findings. We suggest that the metaanalysts seek feedback from colleagues on whether the tables are easy to follow and self-explanatory (as a rule, any table should be understandable on its own, without the reader needing to read the narrative text that supplements the table). As previously noted, we recommend indicating to readers how many of the primary studies contributed to each metacategory (see Chapter 4,

Tables 4.3–4.7). This reference to the primary studies enhances the transparency of a QMA because readers can check the original studies for themselves and determine whether they can locate a finding that the meta-analysts assigned to particular metacategories. We also recommend the use of illustrative quotes from the original studies (it is important here to avoid overreliance on quotes from one specific primary study, unless there is a reason for doing so, and the reason why a particular study dominates the illustrations is fully explained).

A problem shared with individual qualitative studies is that the meta-analysts may be grappling with a large amount of information to present in the Results section. Some of our studies ended up with more than 20 metacategories. It sometimes helps to hierarchically structure the metacategories or to see whether there could be any subdomains present to help you organize data in a more streamlined manner. It may also be useful to explore whether electronic online supplementary material can be submitted with a manuscript. Many journals allow for this and encourage authors to provide such material. The meta-analysts may thus need to decide what constitutes the core of their findings that they will present in the main body of text and which findings may be submitted in an electronic supplement.

DISCUSSION

The Discussion section of a QMA is similar to the Discussion section of any other empirical study: It summarizes the answer that the QMA provides to the research question it posed. The meta-analysts also can situate the findings in the context of the existing knowledge base and the research problem the QMA attempted to address. Given that meta-analysts typically want to provide a comprehensive (summative, authoritative, more definite) picture of a field of study, it is important to convey the main message for the field, theory, future research, and practice (policy) that can then be expanded on. The Discussion section is an opportunity for the meta-analysts to reflect on the strengths of their QMA but also, primarily, on its limitations, and share these transparently with the reader. In discussing the limitations, the meta-analysts should caution the reader about the possible weaker points of the QMA.

We end this section by referring readers to the Appendix, which contains references of exemplar published QMAs from psychology (or that are directly relevant to psychology). We selected some of our own work and some work of other researchers.

SUMMARY

In this chapter, we have outlined, on the basis of our own experience, some points for meta-analysts to consider when trying to publish their QMA. We provided some tips and suggestions for the main sections of a manuscript and outlined the essential information that needs to be included in each section. Research findings across samples and studies are more compelling than those from a single study, so we strongly encourage readers to persevere and publish their QMAs.

7 SUMMARY AND FUTURE DIRECTIONS

In this book, we have presented a rationale for qualitative meta-analysis (QMA) and highlighted specific procedures and steps on how to conduct one. Although we presented all the steps in a linear manner, as with any qualitative research study, QMA is a flexible, creative endeavor that is iterative and can be adjusted when challenges are encountered. Also, the approach we offer is similar to another book in this series (Elliott & Timulak, 2021), which provides an account of a generic approach that does not preclude adjustments to and inspirations taken from more brand name QMA approaches (e.g., grounded formal theory, metastudy, meta-summary). In fact, our approach overlaps with those brand name descriptions and, in a sense, distills a lot of their essence. That distillation, coupled with our personal experience in conducting QMAs, has shaped our descriptions of the process of conducting a QMA.

The goal of this final chapter is to provide a concise summary of the descriptive procedures and steps we have presented. We provide this summary in the format of sample questions that meta-analysts may find useful to reflect on in each stage of the QMA process (see Table 7.1). These questions are based on our experience and lessons we have learned from conducting QMAs. The sample questions are not intended to stifle creativity—the list is not

https://doi.org/10.1037/0000313-007
Essentials of Qualitative Meta-Analysis, by L. Timulak and M. Creaner

TABLE 7.1. Examples of Questions Relevant to a Qualitative Meta-Analysis (QMA)

QMA stage	Key questions
Establishing the need for a meta-analysis	• What is informing your decision to conduct a QMA on this topic? • What is the purpose of the proposed QMA? • Why is the QMA an appropriate methodology? • Will the protocol for the QMA be registered (e.g., PROSPERO)?
Developing a research problem/ guiding question	• What is your research problem, and how does it translate into your research questions? • Can this research question be answered by a QMA? • Is this question, or a similar one, being asked in the literature? Was there any other QMA conducted? • Did you compare your research questions with the guidelines for the development of research questions, such as PICO or SPIDER? • Is the research question flexible enough to be adapted and accommodated, if needed, in light of appraisal of the primary studies?

Identifying and selecting original studies	• How will the original/primary studies be identified?
	• What search terms or key words will be used?
	• What will comprise the inclusion and exclusion criteria?
	  – What date range will be applied?
	  – What is the target population?
	• What search strategy will be used?
	• Will search tools be considered (e.g., SPIDER)?
	• What electronic databases will be used?
	• What additional searches may be required (e.g., manual search of reference lists, books)?
	• Will primary studies be published/peer reviewed?
	• Will unpublished material be included?
	• Will a manual search be undertaken to identify additional studies or nonindexed studies?
	• Will methodologically similar and diverse studies be included?
	• How will the search be recorded and reported?

Appraisal of primary studies	• Do the original studies respond to the QMA research question or questions? • Should methodologically diverse studies be included and analyzed separately?

TABLE 7.1. Examples of Questions Relevant to a Qualitative Meta-Analysis (QMA) *(Continued)*

QMA stage	Key questions
	• What evaluation criteria will be applied to the methodological features of the original studies?
	– Study aims
	– Study context
	– Theoretical framework used
	– Description of sample
	– Data collection methods
	– Data analysis methods
	– Attempts made to establish credibility and trustworthiness
	– Researcher reflexivity
	– Rich data/illustrative quotes
	– Ethical considerations
	• How did these methodological features influence the results of the primary study (and thus the results of the QMA)?
	• On the basis of the appraisal, is there a need to revisit the QMA research questions, inclusion criteria, or evaluation criteria?
	• How will the appraisal be recorded/documented and reported?
Preparing data	• Where are the data in the original study? Were the findings, contextual information, and participant information reported verbatim?
	• Is an original data set available (relevant only for rare cases when a QMA combines data sets)?
	• Are the data in the primary study representative of the primary study's sample (e.g., many quotes from the same participant)?
	• How will you break down the data into manageable chunks (meaning units)?
Data analysis	• What are the domains of the investigation/conceptual framework to organize the data?
	• How are the meta-analysts' theoretical and epistemological positions and professional and personal backgrounds influencing the analysis?
	• How is the analysis congruent with the QMA research question?
	• How well are the primary studies represented in the final QMA analysis?
	• Which meaning units can be clustered together (categorized)?
	• How will a name be chosen for the metacategory?
	• How will findings be organized and synthesized?
	• How do the methodological features of the primary studies influence the QMA findings?

(continues)

TABLE 7.1. Examples of Questions Relevant to a Qualitative Meta-Analysis (QMA) *(Continued)*

QMA stage	Key questions
Credibility checks	• What strategies will be used to enhance credibility, trustworthiness, and methodological integrity? • Will independent auditors/raters or a team consensus be used at all QMA stages? • Will triangulation be used? • How will the representativeness of a metacategory to the sample be evaluated (e.g., how many primary studies contribute to a particular metacategory)?
Presentation of findings	• Are the characteristics of primary studies (e.g., sample characteristics, data collection and analysis methods, pertinent methodological features) clearly presented? • How will the QMA findings be succinctly presented? • Are the findings presented in an accessible and coherent manner? • Will tables or figures be used? Are they self-explanatory? • What informs the use of participant quotes from the original studies? • How well do the selected quotes illustrate the QMA metacategory being presented?
Write-up of the study	• What journals could be considered for publication of the QMA? • What reporting standards are relevant (e.g., QMARS, PRISMA)? • How might the use of tables, figures, and illustrative examples enhance the presentation? • Did the QMA provide a more conclusive perspective on the area/phenomenon of investigation? • What is the contribution of the QMA to new knowledge? • What are the implications, for theory, practice, and policy development? • Will the QMA need to be updated in the future? What factors will inform this decision?

Note. PROSPERO = International Prospective Register of Systematic Reviews in Health and Social Care (see https://www.crd.york.ac.uk/prospero/); PICO = (population, intervention, comparison, and outcome); SPIDER = Sample-Phenomenon of Interest-Design-Evaluation-Research Type (see Cooke et al., 2012; see also Booth, 2016); QMARS = Qualitative Meta-Analysis Article Reporting Standards (see Levitt et al., 2018); PRISMA = Preferred Reporting Items for Systematic Reviews and Meta-Analyses (see Moher et al., 2009; Rethlefsen et al., 2021; https://www.prisma-statement.org/). From "Meta-Analysis in Qualitative Research: A Descriptive-Interpretative Approach," by L. Timulak and M. Creaner, in U. Flick (Ed.), *The Sage Handbook of Qualitative Research Design* (pp. 565–566), 2022, Sage Publications. Copyright 2022 by Sage. Adapted with permission.

necessarily exhaustive, and indeed, they evolve with each QMA. We hope the table conveys some of the spirit of the QMA process. Finally, it offers also some questions that can be useful when preparing a QMA for publication.

FUTURE DIRECTIONS AND PARTING COMMENTS

QMAs in psychology comprise a new area that reflects the stage of development of qualitative research in psychology. We expect that with more QMAs being published in the field of psychology and psychology-related journals, the standards for QMA conduct and publishing will evolve further, as happened with quantitative meta-analysis. It is also likely that QMAs will shed light on the methodological practices in the primary studies and can thus shape the standards of qualitative studies in general. This book captures our perspectives and experiences at this point in time. We are looking forward to methodological discussions with our colleagues, fellow meta-analysts, reviewers of QMAs, and journal editors. For now, we believe we can learn from various disciplines, such as nursing, in which this genre of qualitative research has had a longer tradition. However, with the quality of methodological tradition and the space that is devoted to research training in psychology education, we are confident that psychology as a discipline will be able to offer many insights into the further development of the QMA method that will have an impact across many scientific disciplines.

Appendix

EXEMPLAR STUDIES

Qualitative meta-analysis (QMA) relevant to psychology:

Achterbergh, L., Pitman, A., Birken, M., Pearce, E., Sno, H., & Johnson, S. (2020). The experience of loneliness among young people with depression: A qualitative meta-synthesis of the literature. *BMC Psychiatry, 20*(1), 1–23. https://doi.org/10.1186/s12888-020-02818-3

Theoretically informed QMA published in a mainstream journal that normally covers quantitative reviews:

Almeida, S. N., Elliott, R., Silva, E. R., & Sales, C. M. (2019). Fear of cancer recurrence: A qualitative systematic review and meta-synthesis of patients' experiences. *Clinical Psychology Review, 68*, 13–24. https://doi.org/10.1016/j.cpr.2018.12.001

QMA published in a mainstream journal normally dedicated to quantitative reviews:

Levitt, H. M., Pomerville, A., & Surace, F. I. (2016). A qualitative meta-analysis examining clients' experiences of psychotherapy: A new agenda. *Psychological Bulletin, 142*(8), 801–830. https://doi.org/10.1037/bul0000057

QMA published in the form of a report:

Timulak, L., Buckroyd, J., Klimas, J., Creaner, M., Wellsted, D., Bunn, F., Bradshaw, S., & Green, G. (2013). *Helpful and unhelpful aspects of eating disorders treatment involving psychological therapy: A meta-synthesis of qualitative research studies.* British Association for Counselling and Psychotherapy.

QMA that presents results in the form of narratives:

Timulak, L., & McElvaney, R. (2013). Qualitative meta-analysis of insight events in psychotherapy. *Counselling Psychology Quarterly, 26*(2), 131–150. https://doi.org/10.1080/09515070.2013.792997

Early example of a QMA:

Timulak, L. (2007). Identifying core categories of client identified impact of helpful events in psychotherapy: A qualitative meta-analysis. *Psychotherapy Research, 17*(3), 305–314. https://doi.org/10.1080/10503300600608116

References

Achterbergh, L., Pitman, A., Birken, M., Pearce, E., Sno, H., & Johnson, S. (2020). The experience of loneliness among young people with depression: A qualitative meta-synthesis of the literature. *BMC Psychiatry, 20*(1), 1–23.

Almeida, S. N., Elliott, R., Silva, E. R., & Sales, C. M. D. (2019). Fear of cancer recurrence: A qualitative systematic review and meta-synthesis of patients' experiences. *Clinical Psychology Review, 68*, 13–24. https://doi.org/10.1016/j.cpr.2018.12.001

Atkins, S., Lewin, S., Smith, H., Engel, M., Fretheim, A., & Volmink, J. (2008). Conducting a meta-ethnography of qualitative literature: Lessons learnt. *BMC Medical Research Methodology, 8*(1), 21. https://doi.org/10.1186/1471-2288-8-21

Banasiak, S. J., Paxton, S. J., & Hay, P. J. (2007). Perceptions of cognitive behavioural guided self-help treatment for bulimia nervosa in primary care. *Eating Disorders, 15*(1), 23–40. https://doi.org/10.1080/10640260601044444

Booth, A. (2016). Searching for qualitative research for inclusion in systematic reviews: A structured methodological review. *Systematic Reviews, 5*(1), 74. https://doi.org/10.1186/s13643-016-0249-x

Booth, A., Noyes, J., Flemming, K., Moore, G., Tunçalp, Ö., & Shakibazadeh, E. (2019). Formulating questions to explore complex interventions within qualitative evidence synthesis. *BMJ Global Health, 4*(Suppl. 1), e001107. https://doi.org/10.1136/bmjgh-2018-001107

Button, E. J., & Warren, R. L. (2001). Living with anorexia nervosa: The experience of a cohort of sufferers from anorexia nervosa 7.5 years after initial presentation to a specialized eating disorders service. *European Eating Disorders Review, 9*(2), 74–96. https://doi.org/10.1002/erv.400

Centre for Reviews and Dissemination. (2009). *Systematic reviews: CRD's guidance for undertaking reviews in health care*. University of York. https://www.york.ac.uk/media/crd/Systematic_Reviews.pdf

Chircop Coleiro, A., Creaner, M., & Timulak, L. (2022). The good, the bad, and the less than ideal in clinical supervision: A qualitative meta-analysis of supervisee experiences. *Counselling Psychology Quarterly*, 1–22. Advance online publication. https://doi.org/10.1080/09515070.2021.2023098

Cockell, S. J., Zaitsoff, S. L., & Geller, J. (2004). Maintaining change following eating disorder treatment. *Professional Psychology: Research and Practice, 35*(5), 527–534. https://doi.org/10.1037/0735-7028.35.5.527

Collins, K. M., & Levitt, H. M. (2021). Qualitative meta-analysis: Issues to consider in design and review. In P. M. Camic (Ed.), *Qualitative research in psychology: Expanding perspectives in methodology and design* (pp. 283–299). American Psychological Association. https://doi.org/10.1037/0000252-014

Cooke, A., Smith, D., & Booth, A. (2012). Beyond PICO: The SPIDER tool for qualitative evidence synthesis. *Qualitative Health Research, 22*(10), 1435–1443. https://doi.org/10.1177/1049732312452938

Critical Appraisal Skills Programme. (2018). *CASP Checklist: 10 questions to help you make sense of a qualitative research*. https://casp-uk.net/wp-content/uploads/2018/01/CASP-Qualitative-Checklist-2018.pdf

Cuijpers, P. (2016). *Meta-analysis in mental health research: A practical guide.* Vrije Universiteit Amsterdam.

Cummings, A. L., Slemon, A. G., & Hallberg, E. T. (1993). Session evaluation and recall of important events as a function of counselor experience. *Journal of Counseling Psychology, 40*(2), 156–165. https://doi.org/10.1037/0022-0167.40.2.156

Dixon-Woods, M., Cavers, D., Agarwal, S., Annandale, E., Arthur, A., Harvey, J., Hsu, R., Katbamna, S., Olsen, R., Smith, L., Riley, R., & Sutton, A. J. (2006). Conducting a critical interpretive synthesis of the literature on access to healthcare by vulnerable groups. *BMC Medical Research Methodology, 6*(1), 35. https://doi.org/10.1186/1471-2288-6-35

Eisenhauer, J. G. (2021). Meta-analysis and mega-analysis: A simple introduction. *Teaching Statistics, 43*(1), 21–27. https://doi.org/10.1111/test.12242

Elliott, R. (1999). *Client Change Interview protocol* [Unpublished manuscript]. Department of Psychology, University of Toledo.

Elliott, R., Fischer, C. T., & Rennie, D. L. (1999). Evolving guidelines for publication of qualitative research studies in psychology and related fields. *British Journal of Clinical Psychology, 38*(3), 215–229. https://doi.org/10.1348/014466599162782

Elliott, R., & Timulak, L. (2005). Descriptive and interpretive approaches to qualitative research. In J. Miles & P. Gilbert (Eds.), *A handbook of research methods for clinical and health psychology* (pp. 147–159). Oxford University Press.

Elliott, R., & Timulak, L. (2021). *Essentials of descriptive-interpretive qualitative research: A generic approach.* American Psychological Association. https://doi.org/10.1037/0000224-000

Finfgeld-Connett, D. (2018). *A guide to qualitative meta-synthesis.* Routledge. https://doi.org/10.4324/9781351212793

Finfgeld-Connett, D., & Johnson, E. D. (2013). Literature search strategies for conducting knowledge-building and theory-generating qualitative systematic reviews. *Journal of Advanced Nursing, 69*(1), 194–204. https://doi.org/10.1111/j.1365-2648.2012.06037.x

Fischer, C. T. (2009). Bracketing in qualitative research: Conceptual and practical matters. *Psychotherapy Research, 19*(4-5), 583–590. https://doi.org/10.1080/10503300902798375

France, E. F., Wells, M., Lang, H., & Williams, B. (2016). Why, when and how to update a meta-ethnography qualitative synthesis. *Systematic Reviews, 5*(1), 44. https://doi.org/10.1186/s13643-016-0218-4

Giorgi, A. (Ed.). (1985). *Phenomenology and psychological research.* Duquesne University Press.

Glaser, B. G., & Strauss, A. (1967). *The discovery of grounded theory: Strategies for qualitative research.* Aldine.

Harari, M. B., Parola, H. R., Hartwell, C. J., & Riegelman, A. (2020). Literature searches in systematic reviews and meta-analyses: A review, evaluation, and recommendations. *Journal of Vocational Behavior, 118*(Suppl. 1), 103377. Advance online publication. https://doi.org/10.1016/j.jvb.2020.103377

Harrison, H., Griffin, S. J., Kuhn, I., & Usher-Smith, J. A. (2020). Software tools to support title and abstract screening for systematic reviews in healthcare: An evaluation. *BMC Medical Research Methodology, 20*(1), 7–19. https://doi.org/10.1186/s12874-020-0897-3

Herber, O. R., Bücker, B., Metzendorf, M. I., & Barroso, J. (2017). A qualitative meta-summary using Sandelowski and Barroso's method for integrating qualitative research to explore barriers and facilitators to self-care in heart failure patients. *European Journal of Cardiovascular Nursing, 16*(8), 662–677. https://doi.org/10.1177/1474515117711007

Hill, C. E., & Knox, S. (2021). *Essentials of consensual qualitative research.* American Psychological Association. https://doi.org/10.1037/0000215-000

Hill, C. E., Knox, S., & Hess, S. A. (2012). Qualitative meta-analyses of consensual qualitative research studies. In C. E. Hill (Ed.), *Consensual qualitative research: A practical resource for investigating social science phenomena* (pp. 159–171). American Psychological Association.

Hissa, J., & Timulak, L. (2020). Theoretically informed qualitative psychotherapy research: A primer. *Counselling & Psychotherapy Research, 20*(3), 429–434. https://doi.org/10.1002/capr.12301

Irwin, S. (2013). Qualitative secondary data analysis: Ethics, epistemology, and context. *Progress in Development Studies, 13*(4), 295–306. https://doi.org/10.1177/1464993413490479

Jennings, L., D'Rozario, V., Goh, M., Sovereign, A., Brogger, M., & Skovholt, T. (2008). Psychotherapy expertise in Singapore: A qualitative investigation. *Psychotherapy Research, 18*(5), 508–522. https://doi.org/10.1080/10503300802189782

Jensen, L. A., & Allen, M. N. (1996). Metasynthesis of qualitative findings. *Qualitative Health Research, 6*(4), 553–560. https://doi.org/10.1177/104973239600600407

Kearney, M. H. (1998). Ready-to-wear: Discovering grounded formal theory. *Research in Nursing & Health, 21*(2), 179–186. https://doi.org/10.1002/(SICI)1098-240X(199804)21:2<179::AID-NUR8>3.0.CO;2-G

Kearney, M. H. (2001). Enduring love: A grounded formal theory of women's experience of domestic violence. *Research in Nursing & Health, 24*(4), 270–282. https://doi.org/10.1002/nur.1029

Ladmanová, M., Řiháček, T., & Timulak, L. (2021). Client-identified impacts of helpful and hindering events in psychotherapy: A qualitative meta-analysis. *Psychotherapy Research.* Advance online publication. https://doi.org/10.1080/10503307.2021.2003885

Levitt, H. M. (2018). How to conduct a qualitative meta-analysis: Tailoring methods to enhance methodological integrity. *Psychotherapy Research, 28*(3), 367–378. https://doi.org/10.1080/10503307.2018.1447708

Levitt, H. M. (2019). *Reporting qualitative research in psychology: How to meet APA style journal article reporting standards.* American Psychological Association. https://doi.org/10.1037/0000121-000

Levitt, H. M. (2021). *Essentials of critical-constructivist grounded theory research.* American Psychological Association. https://doi.org/10.1037/0000231-000

Levitt, H. M., Bamberg, M., Creswell, J. W., Frost, D. M., Josselson, R., & Suárez-Orozco, C. (2018). Journal article reporting standards for qualitative primary, qualitative meta-analytic, and mixed methods research in psychology: The APA Publications and Communications Board task force report. *American Psychologist, 73*(1), 26–46. https://doi.org/10.1037/amp0000151

Levitt, H. M., Motulsky, S. L., Wertz, F. J., Morrow, S. L., & Ponterotto, J. G. (2017). Recommendations for designing and reviewing qualitative research in psychology: Promoting methodological integrity. *Qualitative Psychology, 4*(1), 2–22. https://doi.org/10.1037/qup0000082

Levitt, H. M., Pomerville, A., & Surace, F. I. (2016). A qualitative meta-analysis examining clients' experiences of psychotherapy: A new agenda. *Psychological Bulletin, 142*(8), 801–830. https://doi.org/10.1037/bul0000057

Levitt, H. M., Pomerville, A., Surace, F. I., & Grabowski, L. M. (2017). Meta-method study of qualitative psychotherapy research on clients' experiences: Review and recommendations. *Journal of Counseling Psychology, 64*(6), 626–644. https://doi.org/10.1037/cou0000222

Madden, L. (2021). *It takes three to tango: Client's experiences of couple therapy: A meta-analysis of qualitative research studies* [Unpublished doctoral dissertation]. Trinity College Dublin.

Madden, L., & Timulak, L. (2022). *It takes three to tango: Clients' experiences of couple therapy: A meta-analysis of qualitative research studies* [Manuscript submitted for publication]. School of Psychology, Trinity College Dublin.

Majid, U., & Vanstone, M. (2018). Appraising qualitative research for evidence syntheses: A compendium of quality appraisal tools. *Qualitative Health Research, 28*(13), 2115–2131. https://doi.org/10.1177/1049732318785358

Malterud, K. (2019). *Qualitative metasynthesis: A research method for medicine and health sciences.* Routledge. https://doi.org/10.4324/9780429026348

Marren, C., Mikoška, P., O'Brien, S., & Timulak, L. (2022). *Clients' experiences of emotion-focused therapy: A qualitative meta-analysis* [Manuscript submitted for publication]. School of Psychology, Trinity College Dublin.

McCormick, J., Rodney, P., & Varcoe, C. (2003). Reinterpretations across studies: An approach to meta-analysis. *Qualitative Health Research, 13*(7), 933–944. https://doi.org/10.1177/1049732303253480

Methley, A. M., Campbell, S., Chew-Graham, C., McNally, R., & Cheraghi-Sohi, S. (2014). PICO, PICOS and SPIDER: A comparison study of specificity and sensitivity in three search tools for qualitative systematic reviews. *BMC Health Services Research, 14*(1), 579. https://doi.org/10.1186/s12913-014-0579-0

Moher, D., Liberati, A., Tetzlaff, J., Altman, D. G., & the PRISMA Group. (2009). Preferred Reporting Items for Systematic Reviews and Meta-Analyses: The PRISMA statement. *PLOS Medicine, 6*(7), e1000097. https://doi.org/10.1371/journal.pmed.1000097

Moreno, J. K., Fuhriman, A., & Hileman, E. (1995). Significant events in a psychodynamic psychotherapy group for eating disorders. *Group, 19*(1), 56–62. https://doi.org/10.1007/BF01458191

Morrow, S. L. (2005). Quality and trustworthiness in qualitative research in counseling psychology. *Journal of Counseling Psychology, 52*(2), 250–260. https://doi.org/10.1037/0022-0167.52.2.250

Noblit, G. W., & Hare, R. D. (1988). *Meta-ethnography: Synthesizing qualitative studies.* Sage. https://doi.org/10.4135/9781412985000

O'Connell Kent, J. A., Jackson, A., Robinson, M., Rashleigh, C., & Timulak, L. (2020). Emotion-focused therapy for symptoms of generalised anxiety in a student population: An exploratory study. *Counselling & Psychotherapy Research, 21*(2), 260–268. https://doi.org/10.1002/capr.12346

Page, M. J., McKenzie, J. E., Bossuyt, P. M., Boutron, I., Hoffmann, T. C., Mulrow, C. D., Shamseer, L., Tetzlaff, J. M., & Moher, D. (2021). Updating guidance for reporting systematic reviews: Development of the PRISMA 2020 statement. *Journal of Clinical Epidemiology, 134*, 103–112. https://doi.org/10.1016/j.jclinepi.2021.02.003

Paterson, B., Canam, C., Joachim, G., & Thorne, S. (2003). Embedded assumptions in qualitative studies of fatigue. *Western Journal of Nursing Research, 25*(2), 119–133. https://doi.org/10.1177/0193945902250029

Paterson, B. L., Thorne, S. E., Canam, C., & Jillings, C. (2001). *Meta-study of qualitative health research: A practical guide to meta-analysis and meta-synthesis.* Sage. https://doi.org/10.4135/9781412985017

Patton, M. Q. (1999). Enhancing the quality and credibility of qualitative analysis. *Health Services Research, 34*(5, Pt. 2), 1189–1208.

Pawson, R., Greenhalgh, T., Harvey, G., & Walshe, K. (2005). Realist review— A new method of systematic review designed for complex policy interventions.

Journal of Health Services Research & Policy, 10(Suppl. 1), 21–34. https:// doi.org/10.1258/1355819054308530

Pearson, A., White, H., Bath-Hextall, F., Salmond, S., Apostolo, J., & Kirkpatrick, P. (2015). A mixed-methods approach to systematic reviews. *International Journal of Evidence-Based Healthcare, 13*(3), 121–131. https://doi.org/10.1097/ XEB.0000000000000052

Rennie, D. L., Phillips, J. R., & Quartaro, G. K. (1988). Grounded theory: A promising approach to conceptualization in psychology? *Canadian Psychology, 29*(2), 139–150. https://doi.org/10.1037/h0079765

Rethlefsen, M. L., Kirtley, S., Waffenschmidt, S., Ayala, A. P., Moher, D., Page, M. J., Koffel, J. B., & the PRISMA-S Group. (2021). PRISMA-S: An extension to the PRISMA statement for reporting literature searches in systematic reviews. *Systematic Reviews, 10*(1), 39. https://doi.org/10.1186/s13643-020-01542-z

Rorty, M., Yager, J., & Rossotto, E. (1993). Why and how do women recover from bulimia nervosa? The subjective appraisals of forty women recovered for a year or more. *International Journal of Eating Disorders, 14*(3), 249–260. https:// doi.org/10.1002/1098-108X(199311)14:3<249::AID-EAT2260140303> 3.0.CO;2-O

Sandelowski, M. (2012). Metasynthesis of qualitative research. In H. Cooper, P. M. Camic, D. L. Long, A. T. Panter, D. Rindskopf, & K. J. Sher (Eds.), *APA handbook of research methods in psychology: Vol. 2. Research designs: Quantitative, qualitative, neuropsychological, and biological* (pp. 19–36). American Psychological Association. https://doi.org/10.1037/13620-002

Sandelowski, M., & Barroso, J. (2003). Creating metasummaries of qualitative findings. *Nursing Research, 52*(4), 226–233. https://doi.org/10.1097/ 00006199-200307000-00004

Sandelowski, M., & Barroso, J. (2006). *Handbook for synthesizing qualitative research.* Springer.

Schreiber, R., Crooks, D., & Stern, P. N. (1997). Qualitative meta-analysis. In J. M. Morse (Ed.), *Completing a qualitative project: Details and dialogue* (pp. 311–326). Sage.

Smith, J. A., & Nizza, I. E. (2021). *Essentials of interpretative phenomenological analysis.* American Psychological Association. https://doi.org/10.1037/0000259-000

Smith, M. L., & Glass, G. V. (1977). Meta-analysis of psychotherapy outcome studies. *American Psychologist, 32*(9), 752–760. https://doi.org/10.1037/ 0003-066X.32.9.752

Stephen, S., Bell, L., Khan, M., Love, R., Macintosh, H., Martin, M., Moran, R., Price, E., Whitehead, B., & Elliott, R. (2021). Comparing helpful and hindering processes in good and poor outcome cases: A qualitative metasynthesis of eight Hermeneutic Single Case Efficacy Design studies. *Psychotherapy Research.* Advance online publication. https://doi.org/10.1080/10503307. 2021.1934746

Stern, P. N., & Harris, C. (1985). Women's health and the self-care paradox: A model to guide self-care readiness. *Health Care for Women International,* *6*(1-3), 151–163. https://doi.org/10.1080/07399338509515689

Stiles, W. B. (2007). Theory-building case studies of counselling and psychotherapy. *Counselling & Psychotherapy Research, 7*(2), 122–127. https://doi.org/10.1080/14733140701356742

Thomas, J., & Harden, A. (2008). Methods for the thematic synthesis of qualitative research in systematic reviews. *BMC Medical Research Methodology,* *8*(1), 45. https://doi.org/10.1186/1471-2288-8-45

Thorne, S., Jensen, L., Kearney, M. H., Noblit, G., & Sandelowski, M. (2004). Qualitative metasynthesis: Reflections on methodological orientation and ideological agenda. *Qualitative Health Research, 14*(10), 1342–1365. https://doi.org/10.1177/1049732304269888

Timulak, L. (2007). Identifying core categories of client identified impact of helpful events in psychotherapy: A qualitative meta-analysis. *Psychotherapy Research, 17*(3), 305–314. https://doi.org/10.1080/10503300600608116

Timulak, L. (2009). Meta-analysis of qualitative studies: A tool for reviewing qualitative research findings in psychotherapy. *Psychotherapy Research, 19*(4-5), 591–600. https://doi.org/10.1080/10503300802477989

Timulak, L. (2014). Qualitative meta-analysis. In U. Flick (Ed.), *The Sage handbook of qualitative data analysis* (pp. 481–495). Sage. https://doi.org/10.4135/9781446282243.n33

Timulak, L., Buckroyd, J., Klimas, J., Creaner, M., Wellsted, D., Bunn, F., Bradshaw, S., & Green, G. (2013). *Helpful and unhelpful aspects of eating disorders treatment involving psychological therapy: A meta-synthesis of qualitative research studies.* British Association for Counselling and Psychotherapy. https://www.bacp.co.uk/media/1980/bacp-helpful-unhelpful-aspects-eating-disorders-treatment-involving-psychological-therapies.pdf

Timulak, L., & Creaner, M. (2010). Qualitative meta-analysis of outcomes of person-centred/experiential therapies. In M. Cooper, J. C. Watson, & D. Hölldampf (Eds.), *Person-centred and experiential psychotherapies work* (pp. 65–90). PCCS Books.

Timulak, L., & Creaner, M. (2013). Experiences of conducting qualitative meta-analysis. *Counselling Psychology Review, 28*(4), 94–104.

Timulak, L., & Creaner, M. (in press). Meta-analysis in qualitative research: A descriptive-interpretative approach. In U. Flick (Ed.), *The Sage handbook of qualitative research design* (2nd ed.). Sage.

Timulak, L., & Elliott, R. (2019). Taking stock of descriptive-interpretative qualitative psychotherapy research: Issues and observations from the front line. *Counselling & Psychotherapy Research, 19*(1), 8–15. https://doi.org/10.1002/capr.12197

Timulak, L., & McElvaney, R. (2013). Qualitative meta-analysis of insight events in psychotherapy. *Counselling Psychology Quarterly, 26*(2), 131–150. https://doi.org/10.1080/09515070.2013.792997

van Leeuwen, K. M., van Loon, M. S., van Nes, F. A., Bosmans, J. E., de Vet, H. C. W., Ket, J. C. F., Widdershoven, G. A. M., & Ostelo, R. W. J. G. (2019). What does quality of life mean to older adults? A thematic synthesis. *PLOS ONE, 14*(3), e0213263. https://doi.org/10.1371/journal.pone.0213263

Vivino, B. L., Thompson, B. J., & Hill, C. E. (2012). The research team. In C. E. Hill (Ed.), *Consensual qualitative research: A practical resource for investigating social science phenomena* (pp. 47–58). American Psychological Association.

Walsh, D., & Downe, S. (2005). Meta-synthesis method for qualitative research: A literature review. *Journal of Advanced Nursing, 50*(2), 204–211. https://doi.org/10.1111/j.1365-2648.2005.03380.x

Weed, M. (2008). A potential method for the interpretive synthesis of qualitative research: Issues in the development of "meta-interpretation." *International Journal of Social Research Methodology, 11*(1), 13–28. https://doi.org/10.1080/13645570701401222

Zhao, S. (1991). Metatheory, metamethod, meta-data-analysis: What, why, and how? *Sociological Perspectives, 34*(3), 377–390. https://doi.org/10.2307/1389517

Index

About the Authors

Ladislav Timulak, PhD, is a professor in counselling psychology at Trinity College Dublin, Ireland. Ladislav ("Laco"—read "Latso") is course director of the Doctorate in Counselling Psychology. His main research interest is psychotherapy research, particularly the development of emotion-focused therapy (EFT). He is currently developing this form of therapy as a trans-diagnostic treatment for depression, anxiety, and related disorders. He is also researching the use of mental health interventions delivered online. He has written or cowritten eight books, more than 90 peer-reviewed papers, and various chapters in both his native language, Slovak, and English. His most recent books include *Transforming Emotional Pain in Psychotherapy: An Emotion-Focused Approach* (2015), *Transforming Generalized Anxiety: An Emotion-Focused Approach* (with James McElvaney; 2018), *Essentials of Descriptive-Interpretive Qualitative Research: A Generic Approach* (with coauthor Robert Elliott), and *Transdiagnostic Emotion-Focused Therapy: A Clinical Guide for Transforming Emotional Pain* (with coauthor Daragh Keogh) published by the American Psychological Association (2021). Ladislav serves on various editorial boards and, in the past, coedited *Counselling Psychology Quarterly.* He maintains a part-time private practice.

Mary Creaner, Dpsych, is an assistant professor with the Doctorate in Counselling Psychology program and director of the MSc in Clinical Supervision, Trinity College Dublin, Ireland. Mary is an accredited therapist and clinical supervisor with the Irish Association for Counselling and Psychotherapy and works in private practice on a part-time basis. She is also a member of the American Psychological Association (APA) and the Society of Counseling Psychology (APA Division 17). Mary has a keen interest in practitioner research and qualitative research methods and a particular interest in clinical supervision practice, training, and research. Mary has delivered numerous invited keynote addresses, seminars, and specialist workshops and acts as a clinical supervision consultant and trainer to statutory and voluntary agencies. Her publications include the book *Getting the Best Out of Supervision in Counselling and Psychotherapy* (2014). Mary is actively involved in training, research, and practice and presents her research nationally and internationally.

About the Series Editors

Clara E. Hill, PhD, earned her doctorate at Southern Illinois University in 1974. She started her career in 1974 as an assistant professor in the Department of Psychology, University of Maryland, College Park, and is currently there as a professor.

She is the president-elect of the Society for the Advancement of Psychotherapy and has been the president of the Society for Psychotherapy Research, the editor of the *Journal of Counseling Psychology*, and the editor of *Psychotherapy Research*.

Dr. Hill was awarded the Leona Tyler Award for Lifetime Achievement in Counseling Psychology from Division 17 (Society of Counseling Psychology) and the Distinguished Psychologist Award from Division 29 (Society for the Advancement of Psychotherapy) of the American Psychological Association, the Distinguished Research Career Award from the Society for Psychotherapy Research, and the Outstanding Lifetime Achievement Award from the Section on Counseling and Psychotherapy Process and Outcome Research of the Society of Counseling Psychology. Her major research interests are helping skills, psychotherapy process and outcome, training therapists, dream work, and qualitative research.

She has published more than 250 journal articles, 80 chapters in books, and 17 books (including *Therapist Techniques and Client Outcomes: Eight Cases of Brief Psychotherapy*; *Helping Skills: Facilitating Exploration, Insight, and Action*; and *Dream Work in Therapy: Facilitating Exploration, Insight, and Action*).

Sarah Knox, PhD, joined the faculty of Marquette University in 1999 and is a professor in the Department of Counselor Education and Counseling Psychology in the College of Education. She earned her doctorate at the

University of Maryland and completed her predoctoral internship at The Ohio State University.

Dr. Knox's research has been published in a number of journals, including *The Counseling Psychologist, Counselling Psychology Quarterly, Journal of Counseling Psychology, Psychotherapy, Psychotherapy Research*, and *Training and Education in Professional Psychology*. Her publications focus on the psychotherapy process and relationship, supervision and training, and qualitative research. She has presented her research both nationally and internationally and has provided workshops on consensual qualitative research at both U.S. and international venues.

She currently serves as coeditor-in-chief of *Counselling Psychology Quarterly* and is also on the publication board of Division 29 (Society for the Advancement of Psychotherapy) of the American Psychological Association. Dr. Knox is a fellow of Division 17 (Society of Counseling Psychology) and Division 29 of the American Psychological Association.